MW01291160

Stepmom Bootcamp

A 21-Day Challenge

ELIZABETH MOSAIDIS

Copyright © 2018 Elizabeth Mosaidis
All rights reserved.

No part of this book may be reproduced or transmitted in any form or by any means, electronic or mechanical, including photocopying, recording or by any information storage and retrieval system, without written permission from the author.

ISBN-13: 9781730884894

Illustration by Elizabeth Mosaidis

Author Photograph by DM

Author's Note

To protect the privacy of certain individuals the names and identifying details have been changed.

To My Hubby

You fit me perfectly—you are the other half
I never thought I'd find.

My love, my light, and my partner in this adventure.

Acknowledgments

Thank you to my family, friends, and Women With Words writing group for encouraging me to write this book. Thank you for the countless hours that you spent reading my book, editing it, and just listening to me talk about all of my book ideas.

I am especially grateful to my mom for editing my book late at night after I kept sending updated versions of the book.

Thank you to all of you who were brave enough to share your stories with me.

Contents

How to Use This Book:
Read, Take Action, and Reflect

You may be wondering if this book is for you. I wrote this book with the childless or childfree stepmom in mind, but the information can apply to stepmoms or anyone in a stepmom role, whether you are married or not.

If you're looking for a formula to magically transform your life and make everything better, you won't find it here because it doesn't exist. Everyone's stepfamily situation is unique and requires different approaches. However, you will find 21 small steps you can take to provide the foundation for a lasting change. My goal in writing this book was for you to use it as a catalyst for change in your life. Oftentimes, the smallest changes have the biggest impact over time.

Each day, you'll read, and then you'll complete a challenge. Research has shown that when you attempt a big challenge, it can seem overwhelming. However, when you break it down into a series of small steps, that challenge is more achievable. These small steps are known as **bridge challenges** because they bridge the gap between what you see as possible and impossible.

People use different terms to describe this experience–breaking out of your comfort zone or challenging yourself. I believe that when you're challenging yourself or trying something new, real growth happens. And we need to apply this concept to our lives as stepmoms. Have you been thinking about having a tough conversation with your stepchild, but you don't quite know where to start? Have you wanted to plan a vacation with your husband and stepchildren to visit your family, but you don't know if everyone will get along? These are just a couple of examples of scary situations, but there are quite a few out there for stepmoms. Actually, just the thought of becoming a stepmom can be daunting for lots of women out there. Even though these situations are scary, true change and growth can also come out of these experiences. Throughout this book, you will be asked to complete a series of Small Steps Challenges that will help you grow not only as a stepmom, but also as a person.

This is designed as a stepmom boot camp because it will take daily effort on your part. For the next 21 days, I'm asking you to put aside your excuses and simply commit yourself whole-heartedly to completing the Small Steps Challenges. For some of the challenges, you may not want to do them, or you may think, *this won't work for me.* Instead of closing yourself off from the challenge, I encourage you to ask yourself: How can I make this work for me, in my situation? It may take some adaptation or flexibility on your part to fit your unique situation, but you can do it. You just need to be open-minded and have a strong commitment to the process.

After you finish the challenge, take 10 minutes to write and reflect. This will help you process what was helpful and how you might do things differently in the future. You will also see a "Take it a Step Further…" section and this will give you other options for extending the challenge. You can make it part of your daily or weekly routine. Alternatively, you might want to use this book as part of a support group or with another friend, to get together and discuss the ideas. You can also hold each other accountable for completing the daily challenges.

After the 21-day challenge is over, I urge you to continue with the strategies and techniques so you can have a lasting change in your life. It won't be easy, but you can certainly do it. You have two choices: to continue with your life as it currently is or make a change. This is your opportunity to make some changes and transform your life. Let's get started!

Introduction

I'm excited to share my book with you because my passion is educating and empowering stepfamilies. We have so many stepfamilies who are in crisis but don't seek help because they are ashamed or they haven't had any luck with finding resources specifically for stepfamilies. This is surprising, considering the growing number of stepfamilies we have these days. In 1960, only 13 percent of married adults were in a second marriage, but by 2013, that number rose to 40 percent. In fact, 1,300 new stepfamilies form every day.

As you might imagine, it's not easy being a stepdaughter, stepdad, or a stepmom. For instance, only 20 percent of stepchildren reported feeling close to their stepmoms, according to Rachelle Katz, author of *The Happy Stepmother*. You might have personally experienced how that lack of closeness affects relationships within stepfamilies. And I have some other statistics to share with you that show just how hard it is to be part of a stepfamily.

- The divorce rate for second marriages is about 67 percent.
- The greatest predictor of divorce is children from a previous marriage. In fact, divorce rates are 50 percent higher in remarriages with kids than in remarriages without kids.

As you can see from these statistics, we have a growing number of stepfamilies and those stepfamilies are struggling, hence the high divorce rate. That probably doesn't surprise you.

However, I'm going to share some other statistics with you that you probably never would have guessed. Earlier I mentioned the high divorce rate for remarriages with children from a previous marriage. Well, the good news is that if those marriages pass the 3-year mark, they are more likely to survive than first marriages, according to Wednesday Martin, author of *Stepmonster*.

The even better news is if they reach the 5-year mark, they are more likely to survive than any other type of marriage. Researchers attribute this to the extraordinary conflicts the couple overcomes on a daily basis. This strengthens their bond and cements them together.

So the key is to learn how to resolve conflict and take care of problems as they arise. But the issue is that most couples wait too long to get help. On average, couples wait 6 years before seeking marriage counseling. By that time, it could be too late.

To have a successful stepfamily, you need to seek tools and resources to help you navigate your role in the stepfamily. Having resources and a support group might very well mean the difference between a divorce and a happy marriage.

Now, I can tell you from first-hand experience that it's hard being a stepmom, especially the first year. I didn't know any stepmoms, and I was ill-equipped to handle that first year as a stepmom. I was too ashamed to tell anybody at first that I was struggling because I felt like I should be successful. I had married the love of my life and I was successful in other areas, so I thought *why wouldn't I be successful as a stepmom?* I was determined to approach it as I do everything in life–head on, dive right in. Well, I found out later this is one situation where it's better to take things slowly. In general, it takes stepfamilies about four to seven years to blend. And by blend, what I really mean is that's when stepfamilies start to feel comfortable with each other. When I was struggling in my first year, I started looking for helpful resources, but I had a hard time finding any stepfamily resources. That's when I decided to take matters into my own hands.

I went to New York and studied with one of the premier experts in stepfamilies, Dr. Jeannette Lofas, the founder of Stepfamily Foundation. I learned about the unique dynamics that comprise stepfamilies and learned why typical advice for biological families doesn't work for stepfamilies. I became a certified Stepfamily Foundation coach. I wrote my first book, *The Stepmom Project: A 30-Day Personalized Journey,* an interactive book with an action-oriented approach, to help stepmoms navigate their difficult role. While every situation is unique, there are some commonalities and simply knowing someone else is feeling the same way or has been through some of the same struggles can lift the burden of guilty feelings. With this in mind, I wrote this book and built a community so we can help each other to become stronger women and stepmoms together. As Brené Brown says in *Rising Strong,* "We can't be brave in the big world without at least one small safe space to work through our fears and falls." My goal is that this book will help you create that safe space to work through your fears, take steps, and experiment with new strategies to improve your stepfamily life.

Above all, I challenge you to invest in your family by taking one small step each day. As a society, we spend so much time trying to distract ourselves—going to movies, shopping, going out to eat. How much time do you spend working on the relationships within your family? That's where this book comes in. I wish I would have had a handbook to help guide me through the trying times as a stepmom, so that is what I have created for you. I'm asking you to take about 10-15 minutes each day to read through the daily passage, carry out your challenge, write, and reflect. Your strength lies in your willingness to carry out the challenge and to be committed to the process of reading and reflecting each day.

All it takes is a series of small steps to lead to an impactful change. It starts with you.

Day 1: Recognize what you're feeling is normal.

I think this is what we all want to hear: that we are not alone in hitting the bottom, and that it is possible to come out of that place courageous, beautiful, and strong. —Anna White

Do you sometimes feel like an outsider when you're with your stepfamily? Do you wonder if you'll ever fit in? Do you feel frustrated when discussing the children's discipline with your husband? Do you feel resentful when your husband's ex-wife is constantly calling? As stepmoms, we experience countless emotions on a daily basis, but we push aside or suppress them for various reasons. We think we should be better able to handle situations. We think we are the only one feeling the way we do, as if our feelings are odd or abnormal. However, if you answered yes to any of the questions above, you fit right in with the majority of stepmoms. These are all completely normal feelings to have because of the unique dynamics of stepfamilies.

The problem is that, in my work with stepmoms, I've found that nearly 85 percent of stepmoms feel like they're alone. They feel like they are the only stepmom who is struggling. The only stepmom who is feeling frustrated. The only stepmom who is feeling like an outsider when they're at home. The only stepmom who doesn't have it all together.

And what happens when we feel like we're alone? We don't share. We don't talk about how we're feeling because then others will know our shameful secret— they'll know just how ***not okay*** we're doing. They'll think we're a failure. Instead, we keep it bottled up inside and just hope things will get better.

So, how can we combat these feelings? The first step is realizing that what you're feeling is normal. Stepfamilies are different from biological families, and the sooner that you realize that these feelings are common in stepfamilies, and you are not a bad person for having these feelings, you won't be so hard on yourself. You'll be more forgiving of yourself when you're feeling like this. One stepmom to two boys, Lisa, admitted, "I found myself in this vicious cycle. I kept getting angry over petty things, and then I would get mad at myself for being angry about those things. I realized that I needed to stop beating myself up over how I was feeling. Instead, I acknowledged how I felt, allowed myself to feel that way, and reminded myself that it was a normal feeling." By normalizing the way that she felt and not being so hard on herself, Lisa had a much healthier attitude about her stepfamily life.

When I asked stepmoms about some of the challenges they faced when they became stepmoms, I received many responses like these:

- Dealing with feelings of jealousy and trying to figure out how to handle conflict as an adult was frustrating. I was so disappointed in myself for those feelings and didn't know how to cope.

- Adjusting. As a girlfriend, I didn't feel responsibility. As a stepmom, you feel that responsibility.

- I was able to build a relationship with my stepdaughter in the beginning, but the bio mom sabotaged it and made it very hard for me to continue that relationship, so it ended along with her relationship with her dad.

- Being a second wife. Realizing that my stepchild's bio mom will always be in my life and feeling resentful. Feeling like so much of my life is influenced by the other household.

- Blending our families. Finding that balance between being involved and not overstepping boundaries.

- Understanding how my relationship works in regards to my husband and his kids. Trying not to see it as a competition.

- Expressing love and affection with my stepchildren. Trying to build a bond with them.

- The responsibility of an instant family. Balancing discipline and manners that I expected and preferred with what my husband preferred.

- Holidays aren't as much fun. Feeling divided and trying to figure out who has the kids and when.

- Feeling like a "bolt on" family member; not participating in the core group

Once you realize your feelings are normal, the next step is opening up and being honest with yourself and others about how you feel. If you share your feelings, you won't give them an opportunity to fester and turn into resentment or bitterness. Also, remember through trials and tribulations, real growth occurs. Through conflict, we can grow as a person in ways we never imagined were possible. By looking at the positive things that have happened since becoming a stepmom, we can see how our lives have been enriched. Even if you're feeling down right now about being a stepmom, if you dig deep, you can find something encouraging. Uncover those positive feelings because they will help you get through those difficult times. When I asked stepmoms about positive things that happened to them when they became stepmoms, here are some of the responses I received:

- I was never able to have my own children, so I was happy to be a stepparent to fill that void.

- Now that my stepdaughter is older and in college, I really appreciate her for the amazing person she has become. I'm her biggest fan and enjoy the time we spend together.

- I've always wanted kids, so becoming a stepmother has been pretty good. I enjoy the things we do as family. The kids and I have a lot of fun together. They trust me and know they can count on me.

- I've learned how to be a lot more patient and I've also discovered how big children's hearts are.

- My stepchild speaks highly to others of how nice I am.
- The world is not about me. It's about them. I can fill them with love and laughter.

- Marrying the best person in the world and feeling like I am finally at home.

Above all, realizing that you're not alone and sharing your feelings with others will transform the way you feel about being a stepmom. Just knowing someone else shares your feelings will give you a sense of relief and lighten your burden. The problem is that most stepmoms wait until it's too late and then they're feeling completely burnt out. Don't wait until it's too late— acknowledge how you're feeling and share your feelings with others.

Small Steps Challenge: Explore What Being a Stepmom Means to You

Being a stepmom brings up a myriad of feelings due to the complex nature of a stepmom's role. Some might refer to certain aspects of a stepmom's role as a double bind situation, otherwise known as a "no-win" situation. In a double bind situation, a person has a choice between options, but whichever way they choose, they lose out. Philosopher Marilyn Frye describes a double bind as a "situation in which options are very limited and all of them expose us to penalty, censure, or deprivation."

Here are some examples of what this looks like for stepmoms:

- Being a stepmom is helping with homework, attending volleyball games, but not overstepping bounds. Being a stepmom is being a parent, but not too much of a parent.
- Being a stepmom is being too much, and doing too much, but also not being enough, and not doing enough.
- Being a stepmom is feeling like you have to be the bigger person with those who are accustomed to trying to make you feel small.

Your stepmom role can also be full of anxiety and doubt, which looks like this:

- Being a stepmom is feeling like you have to be perfect, but never quite measuring up.
- Being a stepmom is feeling like you're constantly being judged. "Why did you do it like that? My mom always does it like this."
- Being a stepmom is knowing you're right. And then questioning yourself and overthinking your actions.

You might be feeling powerless, like this:

- Being a stepmom is feeling like you're out of control. You can't control how your husband raises his kids because you're not their parent.
- Being a stepmom is feeling like you're invisible at times.

- Being a stepmom is yearning for structure and discipline while feeling powerless.

You could be feeling proud, like this:

- Being a stepmom is feeling encouraged when your stepchild notices and appreciates you.
- Being a stepmom is feeling proud when your stepchild is kind to others.

You might be feeling wistful, with responses like this:

- Being a stepmom is constantly trying, but feeling like it doesn't make a difference.
- Being a stepmom is sometimes wondering, *what if it were just the two of us?*
- Being a stepmom is wishing that you would come first.

These are just some examples of how you might be feeling. Overall, being a stepmom can feel like you're riding a roller coaster with the highest highs and the lowest lows. Your challenge is to get a notebook, set a timer, and write for 10 minutes using the following prompt: "Being a Stepmom is…" There are no right or wrong answers and no judgement. Be honest with yourself and write whatever comes to mind. The most important thing is to write for the full 10 minutes. Through this exercise, you can express all of your feelings about being a stepmom, including those feelings you don't want to share with anyone else. Once you finish writing for 10 minutes, you might find yourself setting your timer for another 10 minutes.

After you finish, choose one or two people and share what you wrote with them. If you don't feel comfortable sharing everything, just share a part of it. You may want to start with a fellow stepmom, but the most important thing is to choose people you can trust. Once you gain more confidence, you should be able to share your feelings more openly with your friends and family.

Take it a Step Further...

This "Stepmom Bootcamp" is not a solo thing–get your husband involved! Chances are good that your husband hasn't read a stepmom self-help book and has no idea what kind of issues you might be struggling with! He also might think issues you're having are unique, which we know is definitely not the case! Ask your husband to read one of your stepparenting resource books so he can understand what you're going through. One stepmom, Lesley, was having difficulty with a cell-phone related issue with her stepsons, so she went to an online forum for stepmoms and submitted her issue anonymously. Fellow stepmoms posted their advice and then Lesley showed their responses to her husband. When her husband saw the responses, he realized that it was a common issue and he figured out the best way to handle it after reading all of the advice. Sometimes it takes an outside perspective, whether it is from a book or an online forum, but the important thing is to get your husband involved.

Reflection

♥ Now that you've finished writing, reread what you wrote. What kinds of feelings emerged as you were writing?

_____

_____

_____

_____

♥ What has helped you get through the difficult times?

_____

_____

_____

_____

♥ How did you feel after sharing your responses? How did the other person react to your responses?

_____

_____

_____

_____

Day 2: Visualize your future self.

When you let go of who you think you are supposed to be, you can become who you want to be. —Shannon Kaiser

As stepmoms, it can be easy for us to get embroiled in what is currently happening in our stepfamily, whether it is a custody battle or disciplinary issues with our stepchildren. We can forget to think about what we want for the future. The custody battle will end, and your stepchildren will grow up, but what kinds of dreams do you and your husband have for the future after your stepchildren have left home? Do you dream about retiring in Mexico, where you and husband will live in a seaside cottage? Or do you picture yourself as an active grandma, taking care of grandchildren and hosting Sunday dinners for the family every week?

One powerful way to figure out where you're going and which steps you need to take in the future is through visualization and then goal-setting based on that visualization. We're going to start by adapting a technique called "Future Self" from the Coaches Training Institute.

Find a comfortable spot to sit and have a notebook and pen nearby so you can take notes. Close your eyes and relax. Take a few deep breaths and focus on your breath. Inhale through your nose and exhale through your mouth. Then imagine that you are going to travel 20 years into the future to visit yourself.

Once you arrive, picture yourself walking up to the house. What do you see? What kind of place do you live in? Notice the details of the house and the neighborhood.

You knock on the door, and your future self opens the door. What does she look like? How does she act? As she greets you and invites you inside, notice what the inside of her house looks like. What kind of feeling do you have as you walk inside?

As you look around the house, take in the details of her home. What kind of furniture does she have? What is sitting on her coffee table or on her mantle in the living room? What is she interested in? What kinds of things do you see in her house?

Imagine she invites you to sit down in her favorite spot and have a chat. You ask her what has mattered to her most over the past 20 years. You listen intently as she shares. Ask her, "What do I need to do to get from where I am to where you are?" Listen carefully and ask questions as she responds.

Ask her, "How has your role as a stepmom evolved?" Be open to listening to her answers, and let her answers surprise you.

Ask her, "What advice would you give to me?" Listen carefully to what she has to say. Be open to her responses.

At the end of your visit, thank her for her support and guidance. You are grateful for her wisdom, and you know that you can return at any time to visit her.

Now open your eyes, and write in detail about what you experienced in your visualization. Make sure to write down feelings, images, and descriptions of your time with your future self. Try to capture what you saw and how you felt.

This woman, your future self, will become your inner mentor and will help guide you in your everyday decisions. Your goal will be to work towards that visualization, and you will ask questions of your inner mentor, who is actually an older, wiser version of you. Use the vision of your life that you experienced to set goals and work towards becoming that woman or stepmom that you want to be. Step by step, start making decisions that allow you to grow into that vision of your future self.

Small Steps Challenge: Visualize and Set Goals

Now that you have completed your visualization, the next step is to set goals to help you become that woman you want to be. Write down at least three specific goals to work on.

Let's imagine that your future self is a self-assured, confident woman who invites you into her home. She lives in a seaside cottage, set high upon a hill overlooking the Pacific Ocean. Her house is light, airy, and welcoming, with bright accent colors such as turquoise and coral. You notice artifacts from her travels around the room. She has pictures of herself and her husband on the beach, as well as pictures of her stepkids and grandkids near a waterfall. She starts talking excitedly about her latest trip with her husband to Macchu Pichu in Peru. She mentions that she is also looking forward to seeing her stepkids and grandkids this summer. They are all getting together at a resort in Zion National Park. They're going to go hiking, fishing, and have s'mores around a bonfire in the evenings. So, in this case, your future self has a healthy marriage and she also has a good relationship with her stepkids. You get the impression that she sees her stepkids and grandkids on a regular basis, and they enjoy their time together. You notice that your future self likes to travel, both with her husband, and also with her stepkids and grandkids. If that's the case, you should set some goals to travel as a couple, and also plan separate trips with your stepkids.

You also notice that your future self seems happy in her marriage. When you think about your current relationship with your husband, you realize that in order to have a happier marriage, you need to have better communication with your spouse about his children. Then that becomes one of your goals that you write down. Or maybe you realize that you're not as loving as you would like to be. So you write down a goal of leaving a love note or giving a compliment every day.

It's important to write these goals down, as research has shown if you write them down, you're 42 percent more likely to achieve them. After you've written them down, ask yourself these two questions:

- How will I achieve this?
- Which steps will I take on a daily, weekly, and monthly basis?

Take it a Step Further...

Another great way to have a visual reminder of your goals is to create a vision board of the life you want to have in the future. You can also get your whole family involved by having everyone make a vision board of their goals for their future.

Reflection

♥ How did you feel about your vision of your life 20 years from now? What surprised you most about your future self?

_____

_____

_____

_____

♥ What do you want to keep in mind for the future?

_____

_____

_____

_____

♥ What did you gain from this experience?

_____

_____

_____

Day 3: Have a tough conversation.

Sometimes all you need is 20 seconds of insane courage—20 seconds of embarrassing bravery and I promise you something great will come of it.
—Matt Damon in We Bought a Zoo

You know the tough conversation I'm talking about. That one you've been thinking about and putting off because you don't know quite how to approach it. I had one recently with my stepdaughter, Emily. I kept going over it in my mind. One of the most difficult things was just figuring how to bring it up. Finally, one day we were making handmade cards together and chatting. I decided it was a good time to bring it up, as we were both involved with what we were doing but still open to having a conversation.

My tough conversation was letting her know how difficult I think it would be to have stepparents and how it's completely normal for stepchildren to wish that their parents would get back together. I didn't want her to feel guilty about having those feelings or to feel like she has to hide those feelings. I told her that I wouldn't have wanted to have stepparents. My parents have been married for 45 years, so I can't imagine what it would be like to have stepparents. Her response surprised me. She said in the beginning it was hard for her, but now she likes having two households. She knows that it's better because her parents are happier now than when they were together. While I appreciated her response, I let her know that even though she may feel like that now, in the future she might feel differently and that's completely normal.

Being part of a stepfamily is difficult for everyone. I think we both felt relieved after having this conversation and I don't know why we didn't have it sooner! Sometimes, we have a tendency to avoid talking about difficult issues because we think it may stir up emotions. However, I felt closer to Emily after we had this conversation, and she seemed to feel more comfortable around me. By opening up a dialogue, you can tackle tough issues and learn more about the other people in your life in the process.

I talked to one stepmom recently who was upset because she had a tiff with her teenage stepdaughter over some sensitive topics related to clothing. When I encouraged this stepmom to talk to her stepdaughter, she hesitated and said she didn't want to because she didn't want to make the situation worse. Once again, I urged her to be honest and let her stepdaughter know that she loves her and just wants the best for her. The next day, she told me how hard it was to bring it up to her stepdaughter, but as soon as she did, her stepdaughter opened up and shared how she felt about the situation. Because of the conversation, they were able to understand the other person's perspective. Both of them felt better after the conversation and the stepmom mentioned she felt closer to her stepdaughter afterwards.

When having a tough conversation, it's important to be open-minded and to listen with a desire to put yourself in the other person's shoes and view the situation from their perspective. In an interview with vulnerability researcher Brené Brown, Michelle Buck, a professor of leadership, emphasizes how crucial it is to try to understand the other person's point of view. Buck explains, "I believe one of the most courageous things to say in an uncomfortable conversation is 'Tell me more.' Exactly when we want to turn away and change the topic, or end the conversation, we have the opportunity to ask what else we need to fully understand the other person's perspective. 'Help me understand why this is so important to you' or 'help me understand why you don't agree.'" Buck emphasizes that after we ask for the other person's perspective, we should stop talking and really listen. Instead of thinking about how we're going to respond, we should listen with the intent of fully understanding that other person's perspective.

Of course, this is not as easy as it sounds, but you can start by practicing it at home. When your stepchild tells you about a problem they had with their teacher or with their friends, instead of assuming what happened or asking leading questions, simply respond with, "Tell me more." Then get ready to listen with your whole heart. Allow your stepchildren to open up to you and share what happened. You might be surprised by how far three little words can open the door to communication.

Small Steps Challenge: Have a Tough Conversation

Your challenge is to think of a tough conversation that you really need to have with your stepchildren, your spouse, or someone else in your life. Decide who you want to talk to and what you want that person to take away from your conversation. Write down what you need to discuss, including a list of the main points, if necessary. Go over what you might say and possible reactions. Now it's time to set a goal for when you will have the conversation. Tomorrow? Next week? Even if it may be uncomfortable, push yourself and get it done. Remember to give the other person an opportunity to tell you more about the situation while you actively listen.

Take it a Step Further...

Think about other tough conversations that you need to have in your life. What type of outcome do you hope to have from these conversations? Be proactive about having these conversations in your life. Also, make it a habit to listen with intention. Encourage others by saying "Tell me more." You'll notice that you'll have more positive interactions with others.

Reflection

♥ Why was this tough conversation important to you? What did you want the other person to take away from your conversation?

_____

_____

_____

_____

♥ How did your tough conversation go? What went well?

_____

_____

_____

_____

♥ What would you do differently next time?

_____

_____

_____

_____

♥ What are some other tough conversations you need to have?

_____

_____

_____

_____

Day 4: Let it go.

You will find that it is necessary to let things go; simply for the reason that they are heavy. So let them go, let go of them. I tie no weights to my ankles. —C. JoyBell C.

Picture a father and two children on one side of the sectional, gathered around a coffee table playing cards. A woman is on the other end of the sectional watching TV, but she keeps looking over at the happy trio. She tries to join in by making comments and encouraging the players, but they give her cursory responses or don't seem to hear her. Her husband's responses are largely drowned out by shouts of, "Daddy, Daddy! Look at me! Look at how well I'm doing!" The woman sighs and turns back to the TV show.

Have you been in a situation like this before where you felt like an outsider? Maybe you felt lonely, isolated, or jealous because your husband and his children were playing a card game and they didn't invite you to join them. Or maybe you felt invisible because they didn't really respond to you. Whatever you might be feeling, you need to recognize that it's a valid feeling that you need to process and work through in order to feel better. You can use the T-R-U-T-H Technique, developed by Tina Gilbertson, a Licensed Professional Counselor and the author of *Constructive Wallowing,* to process your feelings and learn how to let go of them. Follow these steps:

Tell yourself the situation: Recognize what you're going through and why. Think of this as a check in with yourself. Are you feeling like an outsider because your husband and stepchildren didn't invite you to join them? Are you feeling jealous because your husband is giving all of his attention to his children? Recognize what is happening in the situation and what triggered your upset or pain.

Realize what you're feeling: Name your feeling, consider it, and then accept it. You can identify your feeling by finishing the sentence "I feel…" In this case, you might be feeling lonely or left out. Give yourself a moment to consider how you're feeling and then accept it.

Uncover self-criticism: Acknowledge that these are valid feelings, you're in a difficult situation, and you're doing the best you can. Don't indulge in negative self-talk or beat yourself up, which will only result in more negative and bottled-up feelings. A good rule of thumb is if you wouldn't say it to a friend, don't say it to yourself. So, if you're feeling alone, allow yourself to recognize your loneliness and realize that most people would be feeling exactly the same way.

Try to understand yourself: This is an opportunity to connect your present pain to past events that created similar reactions. Have you been left out in other situations in the past? Have your stepchildren ignored you in the past? See if there is a connection with past events.

Have the feeling: Let it move through you completely until it withers away. Allow yourself to feel and process negative feelings. If you allow yourself to process these negative feelings, you can work your way through them.

After following the T-R-U-T-H Technique, I like to add another step, which is:

Self-Reflection: Ask yourself if you can change something in the situation in that moment. Should you wait until a better time? In our example, is the issue better addressed with your husband later? After you give yourself time to process your feelings, think about what kind of action you can take or changes you can make for next time. You won't always need to take action; sometimes you just need to process your feelings, but at least ask yourself if you need to make any changes.

The T-R-U-T-H-(S) Technique is a technique that must be practiced on a regular basis in order to change how you're processing your feelings. The next time you're feeling upset because your stepchild ignored you, or you're feeling resentful because your husband's ex-wife is badmouthing you, take time to go through the steps.

Small Steps Challenge: Make a "Let Go" List

If you're struggling with resentment over issues that keep popping up or maybe you're feeling bitter about how your stepchildren have treated you in the past, it's time to let go of these feelings. Nelson Mandela wrote, "Resentment is like drinking poison and then hoping it will kill your enemies." As painful as these experiences might have been, it doesn't serve you to carry around bitterness, resentment, and anger. Those feelings will weigh you down and affect your emotional well-being over time.

In talking with my coaching clients, I realized this is a common issue among stepmoms. Concrete strategies are necessary to overcome these negative feelings. In addition to the T-R-U-T-H-(S) technique, I discovered another useful strategy in *Adventures for Your Soul* by Shannon Kaiser. In the book, Kaiser introduces the idea of a "Let Go" list, which is basically a list that you create with all of the things, people, and habits that you need to let go of in order to be happy.

To create your "Let Go" list, you should ask yourself two questions:

1. What do I need to let go of?

2. What no longer serves me?

Use the answers to these questions to populate your list. This list serves as a reminder of all those things, people, and habits that are weighing you down and need to be released. Refer to it often as you cross items off your list or add new ones. This is the first one on my list:

1. Let go of feeling that I'm not doing enough as a stepmom. Just being myself and enjoying life is more than enough.

Your challenge is to get a healthy start on getting rid of lingering feelings of anger, bitterness, and resentment by starting a "Let Go" list. See how much lighter you feel!

Take it a Step Further...

Don't forget to continue practicing the T-R-U-T-H-(S) technique in the future as issues pop up. You'll also want to keep your "Let Go" list as a reminder. Look at it each week and see if you need to add anything.

Reflection

♥ How did the T-R-U-T-H-(S) technique work for you? What did you learn?

_____

_____

_____

♥ How did you feel after you completed your "Let Go" list? Were you able to let go?

_____

_____

_____

♥ What do you need to continue to work on?

_____

_____

_____

Day 5: Step back from your stepchild's mom.

Some people and events are difficult to deal with, but they can only stress us if we let them. Breathe in calm, breathe out chaos, and anchor yourself in peace. —Lori Deschene

If you and your stepchildren's mom get along, that's great. If you don't get along, that's okay, too. You might have to come to terms with the fact that you and their mom might not ever get past cordial greetings. As long as your stepchildren see you and their mom treating each other with respect, that is all that matters. Some stepmoms try to push a relationship with their stepchild's mom, but if she doesn't want to have that relationship or isn't ready to have that relationship, don't force it.

In fact, one of the most contentious areas in the lives of a majority of stepmoms is their relationship with their stepchild's mom. Maybe their mom is telling her children negative things about you. Maybe their mom is calling or texting your husband constantly about trivial matters. Or she told the school not to share any information about your stepchild with you. She may be coming over to your house unannounced to see your stepchildren. Maybe their mom keeps asking your husband to come over to fix things around the house. In my work with stepmoms, I've heard a number of situations involving their stepchildren's mom; pretty much anything you can imagine.

For most, one of the biggest struggles is having a high conflict mom in the picture. She could be a person you would never be friends with and you may not like or respect, but you are forever tied to each other. If you want to go on vacation or move away, you and your partner have to work with your stepchildren's mom to change the parenting schedule or custody agreement. She is also a constant reminder of your husband's past. You might feel like you will never be free of her.

While she may be a thorn in your side, remember she is your stepchild's mother, and the better she is as a person, the better your stepchildren will be. If she gets her life together and focuses on her children, think about how much better it will be for the children. If you wish that horrible things would happen to her, remember those horrible things would directly affect your stepchildren's lives. As difficult as it may be, try to step back, distance yourself from her, and focus on your life with your husband and stepchildren.

Reduce or eliminate interaction

When many women become stepmoms, they think they'll have a positive relationship with their stepchildren's mom. They enter the relationship with the best of intentions—they think they will do what is best for their stepchildren, and their mom will do anything she can to help. If you're in that situation, count yourself fortunate, because that is not the case for a majority of stepmoms. In fact, many stepmoms are surprised when the mom rebuffs, ignores, or misinterprets their positive actions. That's when stepmoms need to step back to protect themselves. You can also encourage your husband to limit interactions as much as possible, but it may take some time for him to do that. He is accustomed to his ex's behavioral patterns, so he might not see a problem with it. It may take some time for him to realize that he can stand up to her. Another factor that comes into play is that he might not want to "rock the boat." He may be operating from a place of fear–fear of going back to court for another custody battle or fear of losing his children. Angela, a stepmom of four years, shares her experience with her stepdaughter's mom.

> When I first got married, I felt like my stepdaughter's mom controlled our life. She would call and text my husband a lot, and she would try to tell him what he was going to do or pay for in regards to my stepdaughter. In the beginning, she wanted us to send my stepdaughter back in the same clothes she came in, so I was constantly doing laundry and worrying about which clothes my stepdaughter needed to wear back to her mom's house. When we wanted to change our custody schedule so we could have my stepdaughter more, she resisted. One night, I was feeling particularly bad after she told my husband once again that she would not be changing the parenting schedule. I went to bed wondering if this woman was always going to try to dictate our lives. My husband saw how distraught I was, and he reassured me that things would get better.
>
> After that, we had a turning point in our relationship with her mom. My husband asserted himself when necessary, and he reduced his interaction with her. Rather than calling or

texting, he limited communication with her to emailing. We also changed to picking up and dropping off at school. These changes were better for everyone involved, including my stepdaughter.

This may seem cruel or unnatural to you in the beginning because of course you want to approach the situation with the best possible intentions, but if your stepchildren's mom starts exhibiting negative behavior, such as calling or texting your husband excessively, trying to control him, or harassing you, take immediate steps to protect yourself and your family.

Establish boundaries

If you're dealing with a high conflict mom, you'll need to establish boundaries. If she's calling or texting you, and it's causing stress and anxiety in your life, evaluate whether you need to communicate with her. If not, let her know that you won't be communicating with her unless it's an emergency. You can block her number and her email. Inform her that she can communicate with your husband if necessary.

Many stepmoms have relayed how anxious they feel when they see their stepchildren's mom, or when she calls. Lori, a new stepmom to two girls, explains, "One of my stepdaughters likes to use FaceTime to talk to her mom. Unbeknownst to me, she would set the phone up, and then I would walk by in my pajamas or just after a workout and her mother would be looking at me from the phone. It was invasive—I felt like her mother was in our home. Luckily, my husband felt the same way, and he talked to his daughter about only using FaceTime in her room when she was talking to her mom. That helped immensely." Situations like these cause stepmoms stress and anxiety, and that's when it's imperative for you to set boundaries of what is acceptable.

Emails and texts can be a source of stress and anxiety as well. Think about how easy it is to misinterpret an email from someone you don't like. Now imagine that person doesn't like you as well, and maybe you've been involved in a court battle with this person. How easy would it be for that person to twist the language in your email? "Whenever I would see an email from my stepchildren's mom, I would get a tightness in my chest and feel anxious. Finally, I told her to take me off of her email communications and email my husband exclusively," Lori divulged. Lori felt relieved after she set that boundary. Her husband would let her know about any important emails; otherwise, he handled them. Since he was accustomed to dealing with his ex, it didn't bother him as much as it did Lori.

Use the BIFF Method to respond

When you or your partner receive inflammatory texts and emails from your stepchildren's mom, first decide if it's necessary to respond. Sometimes, their mom might be trying to create drama, or perhaps she thrives off negative attention. She might be unhappy in her own life, and consequently, try to make you unhappy. Just remember that a response is not always required. If you and your husband don't respond to inflammatory texts or emails, she won't have anyone with whom to argue.

A good rule of thumb is to remember you don't have to attend every argument to which you are invited.

If you determine it is necessary to respond, you can use the BIFF method. Billy Eddy, an expert at The High Conflict Institute, developed the BIFF method as a communication strategy for dealing with high conflict personalities. BIFF stands for Brief, Informative, Friendly, and Firm. Here are the foundational aspects behind this method:

- **B**rief: Keep it brief. Long explanations are triggers for high conflict personality types.
- **I**nformative: Focus on the facts. Don't try to argue, share opinions, or defend yourself.
- **F**riendly: Have a friendly greeting (such as "Thanks for responding to my email"); end with a friendly comment (such as "Have a nice weekend").
- **F**irm: Have your response end the conversation. Or you can give two options on an issue and ask for a reply by a specified date.

Let's look at an example of how this may work in your relationship or your partner's relationship with his children's mom.

Email from mom:

"I made a doctor's appointment for Emily on Wednesday after school. I don't know why I always have to do that. Why don't you? Anyway, make sure to put it on the calendar. I don't want to keep reminding you!"

Your Partner's Response:

"Thanks for letting me know about Emily's appointment. I'll send an email to let you know how it went afterwards."

Just remember you don't need to respond to every email or every point in the email. Only respond to what is absolutely necessary, and make sure to follow the steps above. Overall, keep it business-like, document everything, while staying fair and firm.

Be a positive role model to your stepchildren

Part of being a stepmom is being the bigger person with those who are accustomed to trying to make you feel small. By being the bigger person, you don't need to make yourself accessible to someone who is treating you poorly. You still need to take steps to protect yourself by establishing healthy boundaries and reducing or eliminating interaction. The important piece to this is, as Eleanor Roosevelt declared, "No one can make you feel inferior without your consent." You want to be a positive role model to your stepchildren by teaching them values, such as how to treat others. You can always greet their mom when you see her, but you do not need to be overly chatty. Just a simple hello is sufficient.

The other important part of being a positive role model is never speaking disrespectfully about their mom even if she does not afford you the same courtesy. Your stepchild's first instinct will be to defend his or her mother, even if what you are saying is true, so you should never say anything negative about the child's mother. Research has also shown that saying negative things about a child's parent will make the child anxious and affect their self-esteem. The child will wonder if they share the same traits as the parent you are badmouthing.

Parallel parenting is just fine

There is a big push for co-parenting these days, which is great if it works for all parties involved. With *co-parenting*, the two households have open communication and try to have consistent rules and expectations. They discuss issues regarding the children and have frequent contact with each other. They may plan joint birthday parties, go on vacations together, and celebrate holidays together. While this is the ideal situation for the children if all the parents get along, it is also highly likely that it simply won't be possible for you. In that case, you'll want to use parallel parenting.

Parallel parenting is essentially an arrangement in which the biological parents disengage from each other and create their own rules and expectations within their respective households. Typically, the biological parents agree on major decisions, such as education and the custody schedule, but they might have different rules, expectations, and routines between households. They usually celebrate holidays and birthdays separately. While the biological parents are cordial in public, they don't see each other very often, and typically communicate by email. Parallel parenting eliminates high-conflict situations, which is ideal for everyone involved. After years of parallel parenting, the two households may be able to move to a co-parenting model.

Small Steps Challenge: Part 1

The first part of this challenge is to establish boundaries, reduce or eliminate interaction, and work on being a positive role model for your stepchildren. You can also encourage your husband to take steps but be aware it may take time. In addition, he needs to decide that he wants to change his behavior. You can't make that decision for him.

Here is a checklist of ways you can protect yourself and achieve more balance in your life in the face of a potentially contentious relationship. Look through the checklist and decide where you need to make changes.

- Stick to the parenting schedule
- Document everything
- Set boundaries with your stepchild's mom
- Let your husband communicate with his ex-wife
- Block emails or texts
- If you do have to respond to the mom, use the BIFF method
- Be fair and firm
- Change pick-up/drop-off locations to school or a neutral location
- Don't badmouth your stepchild's mom
- Greet your stepchild's mom when you see her

Small Steps Challenge: Part 2

The other part of this challenge is to let go of anger, bitterness, and resentment that you may have for your stepchildren's mom. If you're holding onto anger, it's weighing you down, and then the mom is actually winning. One way you can work on letting go of these feelings is through transactional writing. Write a letter to your stepchild's mom, and after you finish writing, read through it, and then keep it or burn it.

What is transactional writing? Transactional writing is a way of dealing with bad feelings that we cling to or situations that we replay in our minds. It can also cause a shift in our perspective about negative situations involving the mom. Think of it as saying a final goodbye to our emotional baggage, and then sending that emotional baggage on its way, so it is not weighing us down anymore.

How do we do that? The idea is that you write a letter to your stepchild's mom about the situation to try to have some closure on it. You can also use it to try and understand the situation from that person's point of view. After you write a letter to the mom, you can burn the letter to signify the end of your negative feelings or cyclical thinking about the situation. This is a great way to clear the air and move on. If you need some support or motivation to do it, get a group of friends or stepmoms together and write your letters around the fireplace. When I did this recently with a group of friends, we all felt a little lighter and a strong sense of relief after we burned our letters.

Take it a Step Further…

Now that you've finished writing your letter to your stepchild's mom, take a moment to think about past hurts or lingering resentment. Do you need to write another letter to your stepchild or to your mother-in-law? You can keep the letters in a notebook, or you can burn them if that helps you let go of those feelings.

You might even want to write in a journal on a regular basis. In his book *Writing to Heal*, James Pennebaker, a psychology professor, focused much of his research on the healing power of writing. Pennebaker asserts, "Since the mid-1980s, an increasing number of studies have focused on the value of expressive writing as a way to bring about healing. The evidence is mounting that the act of writing about a traumatic experience for as little as 15 or 20 minutes a day for three or four days a week can produce measurable changes in physical and mental health." Pennebaker goes on to explain, "Emotional writing can also affect people's sleep habits, work efficiency, and how they connect with others." Imagine how much better you would feel if you're able to get rid of those feelings of resentment or bitterness.

Reflection

♥ How did you feel after you established boundaries? Did you notice some positive results?

_____

_____

_____

♥ What are some of the other items on the checklist that you would like to try? What is your desired outcome?

_____

_____

_____

_____

_____

♥ How did you feel as you were writing the letter to your stepchild's mom?

_____

_____

_____

_____

_____

♥ How did you feel after you wrote the letter? Were you able to let go of those negative feelings?

_____

_____

_____

_____

_____

Day 6: Be authentically you.

Always be a first rate version of yourself and not a second rate version of someone else. —Judy Garland

Ever feel like you have to act a certain way as a stepmom? Or feel like you can't quite be yourself? Maybe you are putting pressure on yourself to conform to a particular ideal of how you think you should be? Because the very nature of our role is a gray area, tinged in uncertainty, as stepmoms we can start second-guessing ourselves. Or we might become focused on being liked by others in our lives. We want to be liked by our stepchildren, whether we realize it or not. We want to be liked by the other moms on our stepchild's soccer team. We may even want to be liked by our stepchild's mom. (Although we would never actually admit this!)

Along with being liked, comes the praise that we hope to receive from being liked. "You are the best stepmom ever!" we imagine our stepkids exclaiming when we plan a special activity for them. We want to receive praise from our partner for the incredible job that we're doing with their children. "Thanks for helping Emma with that school project. It turned out really well!"

This can send us on a quest for approval and praise, while putting a lot of undue pressure on ourselves. This can even lead us to losing ourselves because we are always trying to please others.

In general, many women are relationship-oriented by nature, so we want to connect and form relationships with people around us, whether those people are our coworkers, neighbors, or our new family. We want to form strong bonds not only with our partner but also with our stepchildren.

The reality is just by the nature of our stepmom role, we won't receive a lot of praise and we're not even necessarily set up to be liked by our stepchildren. With stepfamily dynamics at play, along with strong **loyalty binds** to their biological parents, our stepchildren are programmed to dislike us. It's not that they dislike us *personally*; it's more that they wouldn't like *any* woman who became their stepmom. And if they do start to feel close to their stepmom, they may pull back because of their loyalty bind, or intense inner feelings of loyalty, to their mom. They might feel guilty or may feel like they are betraying their mom if they like their stepmom.

However, it's really hard not to take it personally, and that's when not being liked or not receiving praise can affect our self-esteem. This doesn't just apply to stepmoms. *Anyone* who feels like they are constantly trying to be liked or *anyone* who is hoping for some praise feels the same way.

Unhooking from praise and criticism

You might be wondering how to break this unhealthy cycle of seeking praise from others. Author Tara Mohr offers a powerful strategy in her book, *Playing Big*. She calls this "unhooking from praise and criticism." Mohr offers several principles to help you unhook from praise and criticism, but the one that can really help you is to ask yourself:

- What is more important to me than being praised or liked in this situation?

The answer to this question should remind you of where your true priorities lie. Let's go back to our earlier example of planning a special activity for our stepkids. Ask yourself, "What is more important to me than being praised or liked in this situation?" For me, since my stepdaughter is an only child, I want her to learn how to get along with children her age and make friends, so I try to plan activities like play dates or events where she'll interact with other children. That's where my true priorities lie, and that's where I'll focus my attention.

Or let's say you help your stepchild with a big project at school. Why? Was it because you wanted to receive praise? It's always nice to receive recognition, but I'm guessing most of you would say you helped because you want your stepchild to learn as much as possible and be successful in school.

Asking yourself this question can help you unhook from praise and criticism and reframe the situation so you can focus your attention on your priorities. It will take some practice, but you can do it!

The other part of this equation is recognizing your uniqueness and focus on being yourself. What is unique about you? How can you enrich your stepchild's life? Alice, a stepmother to one teenage girl, loves to cook and host family dinners. Her stepdaughter was more accustomed to dinners-on-the-go rather than having the family gathered around the dining table. However, she was quick to tell Alice how much she enjoyed these meals. What a blessing for Alice and her stepdaughter!

Alice enjoyed cooking for her family, as it was a way for her to express her love, and her stepfamily loved the family togetherness and food at these family dinners. This is one way that Alice could be there for her stepchild without putting a lot of pressure on herself or her family. Just like Alice, you have talents or passions that you probably take for granted, but can help you be there for your new family in an authentic way without putting added pressure on yourself.

Bond over a Shared Purpose

Work on a project with your stepchildren. This could be a volunteer project or a cause in which you both strongly believe. My stepdaughter and I made cards for stepmoms for Mother's day. This was a fun *side-by-side activity* for us, and we chatted while we worked. Side-by-side activities are a good choice for stepfamily members because they can focus on an activity rather than the pressure of interacting "head-on" with one another. Examples include baking, planting a garden, or making crafts. My stepdaughter and I also worked on homemade Christmas gifts for all the family members. We would make one set of gifts for the men/boys and another set for the women/girls. We had a lot of fun choosing the kind of gift we would make, buying the supplies, and then assembling them.

Include Extended Family

Spend time with your stepchildren and your parents, sisters, and brothers. This way, your stepchildren can see you around your family when you feel more relaxed and more like yourself. Just having people who love you and are "in your corner" can help your mood immensely. If family members live far away, try setting up Skype calls or phone calls to keep everyone connected.

When Louise, a stepmom to two girls, traveled back to her hometown with her husband and stepdaughters one summer, they attended a big family gathering with Louise's friends and family members. The room was filled with laughter and camaraderie as everyone chattered and recounted stories from the past. At one point during the evening, one stepdaughter, Ellen, said to Louise, "You have so many good friends and your family is so nice. You belong here." Louise went on to explain that "you belong here" was said in a complimentary way. Ellen finally saw her in a place surrounded my friends and family, and she could see how many friends Louise has and how she fits in with her family. Ellen saw how much Louise's family loves her. Louise also felt more comfortable around her family and friends, so she could be herself, and open up.

Often, as stepmoms, we might feel like we're walking on eggshells. We have to be careful of what we say so we don't offend someone. Having family members around can defuse some of the tension and help your stepchildren see and appreciate you for who you are. When Louise was with her family, she could let down her guard and be herself. Her stepdaughter finally saw her in a new light.

Small Steps Challenge: Make a List

Make a list of 5 things that you enjoy doing or that other people regularly compliment you on. Do you have a talent for finding fun things to do on the weekend? Are you good at playing a sport that your stepchildren like? Do you enjoy baking or making a special breakfast on the weekends? What kind of projects do you like to work on? How can you involve your extended family?

Write these things down and start incorporating them into your stepfamily life on a weekly basis. This week, start with the first one on your list. Next week, you'll move onto the second item on your list. This will not only give you something to look forward to, but it will also help you and your stepchildren bond over something you enjoy doing. They will get to know you and appreciate your unique talents.

Reflection

♥ What is more important to you than being praised or liked as a stepmom? What do you want to focus on?

_____

_____

_____

_____

♥ How did your stepchildren respond to the activities that you incorporated into the week?

_____

_____

_____

_____

♥ How did you feel about the activities? Did you feel more like yourself?

_____

_____

_____

_____

♥ What would you like to try next time?

_____

_____

_____

_____

♥ How do you keep your extended family members involved?

_____

_____

_____

_____

Day 7: Revisit rules and expectations.

Families are the compass that guides us. They are the inspiration to reach great heights, and our comfort when we occasionally falter.
—Brad Henry

Have you ever had a boss that you could not please, no matter what you did? You felt like you were doing the right thing, but then it seemed as though your boss wasn't happy with you? You tried and tried, but it wasn't what your boss wanted. To top it all off, you didn't know exactly what your boss wanted because you didn't have a clearly defined role. Your boss didn't communicate expectations or tasks to you, so you didn't know what to do.

Now imagine that you have two bosses and you alternate weeks with your bosses. So you have one week with a boss who likes things done a certain way, and just when you get used to how this boss likes things done, it's the next week, and you have your other boss. Now you need to remember how this boss likes things done and you need to adjust your attitude to meet your other boss's expectations. After a while, you get used to it, but it takes some time, and you feel exhausted from the extra effort you need to put in so you can please both of your bosses.

This may be how our stepchildren are feeling as they move back and forth between households. Just as you would appreciate some empathy as you moved back and forth between workplaces, your stepchildren would also appreciate some empathy and understanding, along with clear expectations at both households. Everyone works better when they have clearly defined roles and tasks; when they know exactly what they're supposed to be doing. This will take some time to develop, but if everyone knows what is expected of them, they'll be better able to meet your expectations.

That's why it's important for you to have clearly defined rules, consequences, and expectations at your house. First, you need to have a conversation with your partner and make sure you're on the same page in terms of rules, consequences, and expectations. You can ask your stepchildren for their ideas when you're drafting the rules, but you and your partner should have final say.

Don't be surprised if your husband is more lenient than you when it comes to discipline. This is very common with divorced dads and it is called **_guilt parenting_** or **_Guilty Father Syndrome_**. Guilt parenting happens when the biological parent is operating from a place of fear, such as a fear of losing his or her children. Your husband may be trying to please his children because he wants them to enjoy coming over. He may be worried that if they don't like coming over, they might try to live at their mom's house full-time. He may think that since the children aren't with him very much, they should just enjoy their time together and he shouldn't try to discipline them or give them chores.

Consequently, he doesn't discipline them and he doesn't give them chores. As we know, this creates tension in the home when we're dealing with spoiled children. And your husband will likely think that you are too tough. This is part of the dynamics of stepfamilies because we see our stepchildren through the lens of a stepparent, while our husband is looking at them through the lens of a parent. He might overlook some of those small things that bother us. And that guilty parenting could be at play.

If you already have rules in place, evaluate what is going well and what needs to be adjusted as your stepchild is growing up. Think of rules and expectations as constantly evolving and changing depending on the needs of your stepchild and changes to the household or schedule. Naturally, you will have some basic rules related to manners that don't change, but some of the other rules and expectations will change as your stepchild gets older.

After you have your agreed-upon rules and expectations, it is time for you and your husband to present them as a united front. Call a family meeting and go over the rules. Presenting them as a united front is especially important so that your stepchildren know that you and husband agree on the rules and both of you will be enforcing them. Then you can post them up in a place that everyone sees on a regular basis. We posted my stepdaughter's rules up on the fridge, but you can put them on a whiteboard or post them up in the bedroom. Having the rules and consequences posted is a great visual reminder for your stepchildren. This will also make it easy for you when you are disciplining the child. You can point out the posted rules and consequences, taking any argument out of the equation. If your stepchildren protest, you can simply point to the respective rule and say, "Remember our house rules. We tell the truth in our house." Then you can refer to the corresponding consequence.

Manners

One of the most important expectations is related to basic courtesy, and it may seem simple, but it is often overlooked or ignored. In our house, everyone says hello, goodbye, please, and thank you. That means when someone comes home or leaves the house, you should greet someone or say goodbye.

As a stepmom, I'm certain you've had experiences when you felt like you were invisible. One stepmom, Kelly, described a situation in which she went to the pool with her husband to pick up her stepdaughter and a friend. "When we got to the pool, my stepdaughter saw my husband and excitedly yelled, 'Hi Dad!' as she hurried over to us with her friend. She didn't say anything to me and didn't even look at me. It's as if I wasn't there." Kelly went on to explain, "It seems like a minor thing—saying hello to someone. It's one of those little things that most people take for granted until they aren't greeted or even acknowledged." Many of the stepmoms that I have worked with have had similar feelings. Whether your stepchildren consciously or unconsciously ignore you, it still hurts. It is important for you and your husband to address this behavior, and let your stepchildren know that it's common courtesy to say hello, goodbye, please and thank you to everyone.

Another strategy you can try is giving them an opportunity for a "Do-over." If your stepchildren don't greet you when you walk into the room, you can say,

"Oops, you forgot to say 'Good morning.' Let's try this again." Then you can leave the room, and come back in. Hopefully, they'll be ready for a fresh start.

These are important lessons in how humankind works—the way someone treats you is more about them than it is about you. Since you want your stepchildren to exhibit common courtesy and kindness, it'll be important for you to model this behavior and expect the same from them. Your husband needs to reinforce this and have a talk with his children if they're not following the basic rule of saying hello, goodbye, please, and thank you. If your husband is oblivious to the fact that his children are ignoring you, talk to him later and let him know how it made you feel. Then make sure that everyone knows your household rule—we say hello, goodbye, please, and thank you in this house.

Small Steps Challenge: Set Rules and Expectations

Your challenge is to talk to your husband and get a set of rules and consequences drafted up. If you have time today, you can present them as a united front to your stepchildren. If not, plan a family meeting one night so you have time to go over them. Remember that having these rules in place will make it easier for everyone to know what to expect in your household. You can explain how it will be better for the whole family. You'll want to emphasize the important rule: We say hello, goodbye, please, and thank you in this house. The last step is to post the rules, expectations, and consequences up in a visible place. You can even get your stepchildren involved by having them make a sign with the rules.

Reflection

♥ How did your husband react to your discussion about family rules and consequences? Does he suffer from guilt parenting?

_____

_____

_____

_____

♥ How did your stepchildren respond to the family meeting about rules? Is there anything you would change or add, based on their responses?

_____

_____

_____

_____

♥ Have you ever felt invisible around your stepchildren? If so, how did you approach it? Which strategies did you use to overcome it?

_____

_____

_____

Day 8: Incorporate family chores into your household routine.

Every child must have chores to do. It gives them dignity in work and the joy of labor. —Earl Hamner Jr.

As a stepmom, you might go from having just you and your husband in the house one week to having your three stepchildren and your husband the next week. Having your stepchildren adds extra errands and chores to the household for the week, which can add stress if you're not prepared for it. You need to make sure you have enough food for the week, including food for snacks and lunches. Laundry needs to be done and the house should be picked up. What can happen is that you start taking on everything, and then you get stressed out because you still have your regular workload.

You need to start by redistributing the work so that you're not doing everything. Everyone should have designated chores within the household. Your stepchildren are perfectly able to help, and research has shown that having children do chores provides a sense of belonging to the family. Instead of feeling like guests who are visiting, they will feel a sense of responsibility within the household. They will feel better about themselves because they are accomplishing things to help the family, and they will feel a sense of pride when you praise them for the wonderful job they did on raking the leaves or dusting the furniture.

Mealtimes are usually a busy time, with setting the table, serving the food, and cleaning up afterwards. Instead of doing everything yourself and feeling stressed out in the process, give everyone a small job or task. One child can set the table while another one cleans up afterwards. You can even get kids involved in helping with meal preparation. One of our favorite family meals to have is a pot roast in the Crock Pot, especially in the wintertime. My stepdaughter and I enjoy cutting up the celery, carrots, and potatoes the night before, while my husband is in charge of putting it all in the Crock Pot. This meal is about more than just the food–it's also about bonding over the preparation of the meal.

For those with older stepchildren, you can have them get involved in planning or making the meal. I've found that when my stepdaughter makes the meal, she looks forward to trying it, and she thinks it's delicious. I like to think of how this will benefit her in the future, when she is on her own in college or living with a roommate. She'll have some valuable life skills.

As far as an allowance, you and your partner will have to decide on whether you would like to give one. One strategy that has worked well for stepfamilies is for the children to have regular chores without receiving an allowance, but having a list of extra chores that they can do to earn money. That way, if they want to buy something expensive, they can do extra chores to earn the money to pay for it. They'll be learning how to work hard to earn something, and they'll appreciate it that much more.

A key point for the chores is that you and your husband must agree on what needs to be done first before presenting them to your stepchildren. Then you should have them posted up so everyone needs to do what they're doing and when. Instead of constantly reminding your stepchildren of their chores, let them know what the consequences are if they don't do their chores. For instance, my stepdaughter's weekday chore is to do the dishes after dinner and prepare her lunch for school the next day. My husband and I don't remind her to do this on a daily basis. If she forgets to pack her lunch, she won't have one, and if the dishes aren't done before she goes to bed at night, she'll be punished the next day. This way, your stepchildren know their chores and you don't have to keep reminding them. They'll have logical consequences if they decide not to do their chores.

Small Steps Challenge: Create a Chore List

Look around your house and figure out what needs to be done on a daily, weekly, and monthly basis. You might have smaller weekday chores, and then a longer weekend list. Draw up a list of the chores and allowance specifications if you're going to give an allowance. Go over the list with your husband before you present it to the children and post it up.

Reflection

♥ What kinds of chores did you do when you were growing up?

_____

_____

_____

♥ Looking back now, which chores did you find useful to know or learn?

_____

_____

_____

_____

♥ Were there any chores that you wish you would have done when you were growing up? What were they? Could you have your stepchildren do them?

_____

_____

_____

_____

♥ How did your stepchildren respond to the chores? Did you notice any differences in their behavior?

_____

_____

_____

♥ How did you feel after your stepchildren started doing chores?

_____

_____

_____

Day 9: Have fun in your role.

It's not the load that breaks you down. It's the way you carry it.
–Lou Holtz

One stepmom, Helen, expressed how she was having difficulty in her role as a stepmom because she was staying home with her stepdaughter while her husband worked. Since she was staying home with her stepdaughter, she was helping her stepdaughter with homework, making sure that she brushed her teeth and made her bed. All of the things that parents do, but aren't so much fun. When her husband came home from work, he would spend some time reading to his daughter or playing a game with her. Helen started feeling like she wasn't any fun. She felt like she was in charge of forcing her stepdaughter to do all of these things, while her husband got to be "the fun parent." When Helen became aware of this, she started leaving some of these tasks for when her husband got home. Helen's stepdaughter would still work on her homework after school, but Helen instructed her to leave the problems that she had questions on until her dad got home. This balanced things out, so Helen's husband could take on some of the responsibility and it gave Helen a little more time to do something fun with her stepdaughter.

Another stepmom, Rachel, mentioned that she was so exhausted from balancing her work and family life that she noticed that she didn't laugh as much as she used to. Actually, she is not alone, as some researchers have estimated that a typical adult laughs about 17 times a day, while a child laughs over 400 times a day. Rachel felt exhausted most of the time, so she didn't spend time playing with her stepdaughters because she was so focused on the tasks at hand: meals, bath time, and getting them ready to go to daycare. She forgot how to have fun. This absence of laughter in her life struck her one day as she was watching her sister play with her dog, just chasing him around and laughing uncontrollably. *When was the last time I laughed like that?* she asked herself. At that moment, she knew she needed to make some changes to enjoy the little things in life. She decided to become intentional about how she spent time with her stepdaughters. During the busy workweek, she set aside 10 minutes every night to interact with them in a fun way, whether it was playing a game or reading together. She noticed an improvement in her mood and her relationship with her stepdaughters pretty quickly. She also made an effort to do something fun every day, whether it was dancing to a song while getting ready in the morning, singing a silly song, or sharing a funny story from her childhood with her family.

Small Steps Challenge: Lighten Up

When was the last time you really laughed? When I say laughed, I mean a deep, belly laugh. The kind where you're laughing so hard, you're crying. If you can't remember the last time you laughed like that, don't worry. We're going to change that. Think of something fun or silly that you enjoyed doing when you were growing up or before you got married. Did you like to sing in the shower? Tell jokes? Dance around your room when a good song came on the radio? Today your challenge is to do something fun or silly or something that brings you joy. Chase your dog around the house, play a game with your stepchildren, or have a dance party after dinner. Get your whole stepfamily involved and spend at least 10 minutes not worrying about homework, chores, or "To-do" lists.

Take it a Step Further...

It's easy to get caught up in the mundane tasks of everyday life. Be intentional about having fun each week with your stepchildren. If you have more time on the weekend, go to a movie or an improv show. Surprise everyone with an impromptu picnic.

Reflection

♥ When was the last time you really laughed together as a family? What were you doing?

_____

_____

_____

_____

♥ What do you enjoy most about being a stepmom? What are some of the rewards of being a stepmom?

_____

_____

_____

Day 10: Strengthen everyday communication.

Ultimately the bond of all companionship, whether in marriage or in friendship, is conversation. –Oscar Wilde

As the stepmom, you are going to play a big part in building the family unit and setting the tone for your stepfamily environment. Remember that stepfamily dynamics are different from biological families, so you shouldn't have the same expectations for your stepfamily that you would have for a biological family, but you can still build the family unit in authentic ways. While keeping your expectations reasonable, concentrate on what is in your control and possible for you and your stepfamily.

Building trust and having transparent communication are key to strengthening the family unit. If you have teenagers in the house or if you have uncommunicative stepchildren, everyday conversation may be a struggle and that's okay. Remember that you have to start somewhere and you can only concentrate on what is in your control. One stepmom, McKayla, wanted to encourage open communication among her family members. She was hoping to get past the usual mundane chitchat, such as "How was your day?" So she printed off a list of conversation starters, cut them into strips, and put them in a Mason jar. Every night after dinner, one family member would draw out a question for everyone to answer. In the beginning, some of the teenagers grumbled a bit, but after a while, her family started lingering longer to discuss the questions instead of disappearing right after dinner. Everyone started to look forward to the conversation time after dinner.

Another tip is instead of asking your stepchildren for details about their day, tell them about your day. Chances are they'll end up sharing some tidbits from their day rather than one-word responses. They'll also get to know you better without having to ask you a lot of questions.

Small Steps Challenge: Try an Improv Technique

While I was participating in an Introduction to Improv workshop recently, I realized that we can apply some of the techniques within stepfamilies to help build trust and open communication. Our improv leaders at JesterZ Improv in Arizona led us through a series of exercises to put us at ease and to teach us some of the basic principles of improv. In fact, I left the workshop wanting to apply the techniques immediately to my stepfamily life. Your challenge for today is to choose one of the techniques below and try it out with your stepfamily. You may need to modify it to fit your stepfamily dynamics, but the most important thing is just to experiment and have fun with it.

Three Improv Techniques to Improve Stepfamily Communication

   1. **"Yes, and…"**

With improv, you are working with a group of people together to create a scene. Being able to collaborate is important, so the "Yes, and…" idea is exactly what it sounds like: when someone offers an idea, you listen and add another idea. Instead of saying, "Yes, but…" which shuts that person's ideas down, try accepting the other person's idea and adding to it. One little word can make such a difference!

Try it out!

On a family outing, let family members know that you'd like to try something new and the rule for the next hour (or five!) is that instead of saying "Yes, but…" to someone's idea, say "Yes, and…" Talk to them about the importance of working together as a family team and building each other up. Their response might surprise you!

2. **Listen**

When you're part of an improv skit, you have no idea what is going to come out of the other person's mouth. And you need to know what they are going to say because they'll give you clues about the scene: where you are and who you are. This means you need to listen carefully and then respond. You can't plan what you're going to say while they're speaking.

How often do you halfheartedly listen to what your stepchildren or spouse say, but spend most of the time planning what you're going to say? Imagine the impact if you were more intentional about actively listening to them.

Try it out!

One exercise that you could try out with your stepfamily is the "one word story." The rules are simple: with a partner, you tell a story using only one word at a time. One person starts by saying a word and the other person listens and then continues the story by saying a word. What you'll notice is that you can't really plan what is going to happen in the story because you don't know what the other person is going to say. This is also a great exercise in letting go of control because you have no control over where the story will lead. The story will have twists and turns because you and your partner are working together to create it.

3. **Live in the moment**

In an improv skit, you're fully present in that moment. You're engaged in the exchange between you and the other people on stage. You're not concerned about what happened in the past or what will happen in the future. Who knows WHAT will happen next? That's all part of the beauty of improvisation! What would happen if we applied this concept to our stepfamily life? How would our exchanges with our stepfamily members improve?

Try it out!

When you're having a family meal, have everyone put their cell phones away. Don't worry about taking pictures or posting to Instagram. Share what you enjoy about each person or what you enjoy about that moment. Try doing this more often when you're together as a family.

Take it a Step Further…

Overall, I loved the central idea of collaboration over competition in improv. If we apply this idea to our stepfamily interactions, our relationships will improve. Think about how we could build each other up rather than tear each other down. Set aside some time next week or next month to try one of the other techniques. You can also start a Mason jar with the conversation starters for after dinner.

Reflection

♥ How did your family members react to the technique that you chose?

_____

_____

_____

_____

_____

♥ Have you noticed any differences in your family after trying these communication techniques?

_____

_____

_____

_____

_____

Day 11: Be more intentional about creating family traditions.

A family stitched together with love seldom unravels.
–Letty Cottin Pogrebin

Family traditions are very important because they are the glue that bonds us together. If you think back to your childhood, what were some of your family traditions? I'm sure you have some vivid memories of those family traditions. When you join a stepfamily, some of those family traditions might have been established either with your husband and his children or with you and your children. Get your family together and talk about their favorite family traditions. You'll want to discuss which ones are important to keep, which ones you can meld, and possible new family traditions.

Some traditions will happen organically, while others need a little push from you to get started. (And that's perfectly acceptable!) The important thing is to get those traditions started. When you're thinking about what kind of family traditions, think about values. What kind of values do you want to instill in your stepchildren? Lucy, a stepmother to a 10-year-old girl, wanted to emphasize the importance of love, family, and God before material things. Lucy was getting concerned about her stepdaughter's fixation on clothes, jewelry, and tech gadgets, so Lucy decided to establish a family motto tradition each week. Every Sunday, Lucy or one of her stepchildren would choose a quote for the family to focus on and remember each week. Then she wrote the quote down on a chalkboard that was displayed in the living room on the entertainment center. Family members saw the quote all the time.

Your tradition might be to have family photos taken together every year, which is a great visual memento of your time together on a family vacation or on a particular holiday. My husband, stepdaughter, and I unconsciously started the tradition of taking a picture in front of our Christmas tree every year with our dog and cat. In the beginning, we all dressed up in Santa hats or elf ears, with reindeer antlers for our dog. We used that photo for our Christmas cards. One year, we moved into a new house right before Christmas, so I was preoccupied with moving and had forgotten about our family photo in front of the Christmas tree. But my stepdaughter remembered! She innocently asked when we were going to take our photo in front of the Christmas tree. At that moment, I realized she enjoyed this tradition and it was important to her, too.

Another tradition that you can start is celebrating National Stepfamily Day, a nationally recognized holiday that falls on September 16th. National Stepfamily Day is a day set aside to spend with your stepfamily, whether you have a family picnic or go to the park together. Christy Tusing-Borgeld, the founder of National Stepfamily Day, started it in 1997.

When I had the opportunity to interview Christy, I asked her what prompted her to start National Stepfamily Day. She immediately exclaimed, "A lot of heartache! Dealing with ex-spouses on both sides. At first, we all merged together just fine. After a few years, things became incredibly hard. I was on the computer one night looking for some help and support for our stepfamily, and there just wasn't a lot out there. I also noticed that night that President Clinton proclaimed 'National Parents Day.' This sparked the fire. I went to bed that night telling my husband that there should be a National Stepparents Day. But the more I thought about it, I wanted to include all the family members in such a day. So National Stepfamily Day was conceived." Christy is the perfect example of someone who took a difficult experience and turned it into a positive one to help others. You can also spend a positive day together celebrating with your family. Your family might be comforted to know they aren't alone, and there is a special day set aside for stepfamilies.

Small Steps Challenge: Brainstorm Family Traditions

What's your wish for your family? Could you establish a family tradition to help you achieve that wish? Do you want to establish a tradition to help instill certain values? Your challenge today is to make a list of possible family traditions. You can also get your family members involved by asking about traditions that are important to them, and then gather some ideas for new family traditions.

What kind of traditions do you currently have in place? Print pictures from these traditions and put them up around the house. It's wonderful to have visual reminders of the fun times that you've spent together.

Take it a Step Further...

Here are some other ideas that you can work on over the next few weeks to get not only your immediate family involved, but also extended family members as well:

- Get family pictures taken and display them around the house.
- Start a photo album for birthdays, holidays, or vacations together.
- Put pictures of extended family members, such as grandparents, aunts, and uncles, around the house. If extended family members live out of state, make a conscious effort to plan phone calls on a regular basis.

Reflection

♥ How did your new family tradition go? What was the best part?

_____

_____

_____

♥ How did your family members react to your new family tradition?

_____

_____

_____

_____

Day 12: Encourage empathy and kindness.

I find the best way to love someone is not to change them, but instead, help them reveal the greatest version of themselves.
—Steve Maraboli

Are you struggling with kindness and empathy in your household? Do you feel like your stepchildren could use a lesson in kindness and empathy? According to studies in brain and behavior, IQ accounts for only about 20 percent of a child's success in life. The remaining 80 percent is determined by factors related to emotional intelligence, such as empathy, kindness, and gratitude. This is why it's so important to start encouraging skills that foster empathy, kindness, and gratitude as soon as possible.

A little kindness can go a long way in a household that is already experiencing stepfamily stress. If you think about it from the child's perspective, they are going back and forth between two households, and they are probably used to being the center of attention at each household. Having so much attention showered on them doesn't foster kindness or even encourage them to think about others. Instead, it encourages the "me, me, me" attitude of an already selfie-fraught generation. Or maybe the children have been caught in the middle of conflicts between the two households. They might have heard their parents badmouthing each other, or their parent and stepparent fighting. They might not even see their biological parents ever speak cordially to each other. Of course, this environment doesn't model kindness or empathy either. So the question is: How can we raise empathetic children within a stepfamily?

I have six tips to share with you, but remember that every situation is different, so the first thing you must recognize is that you can only do what is within your control. If you and your spouse don't agree on parenting styles, and it's causing a lot of stress in your relationship, then it's time to focus on what you can control. If you think that your stepchild is lacking in kindness, but your spouse doesn't see it, don't keep forcing the issue. Instead of arguing about it or trying to make sweeping changes within your stepfamily, start by following the tips below and repeating them. Over time, you will notice a difference in your children and stepchildren.

Tip #1: Lead by Example

This may sound simple, but this is probably going to be the most difficult one. Take a long, hard look at yourself. Have you been modeling the behavior you want to see in your stepchildren? According to vulnerability researcher and author Brené Brown, "Who we are and how we engage with the world are much stronger predictors of how our children will do than what we know about parenting." That's why you'll want to weigh your actions and decide: if you want your stepchild to be the bigger person, are you modeling that behavior in your relationships? Look at your own behavior and decide what kind of action you need to take. Amelia Earhart best sums this up with a quote, "No kind action ever stops with itself. One kind action leads to another. Good example is followed. A single act of kindness throws out roots in all directions, and the roots spring up and make new trees. The greatest work that kindness does to others is that it makes them kind themselves."

Tip #2: Start a Stepmom/Stepchild Book Club

One question that I get from many of the stepmoms I work with is: what is the best way to connect with my tween stepchildren? First of all, it's not always easy to connect with your stepchildren, especially if you feel like you don't have a lot in common. You can certainly make an effort to find something in common, but don't put a lot of pressure on yourself or on your stepchildren if it's just not happening right away. However, one powerful way I've found to connect with tween stepchildren is through a stepmom/stepchild book club. This is a great way for you to bond with your stepchildren and discuss topics in a low-pressure environment. You can organize a stepmom/stepchild book club or you could have a family book club. The important thing is to choose books that open up a dialogue on kindness and empathy.

I recently organized a summer book club for stepmoms and stepchildren. We read *Wonder*, a book that inspired the Choose Kindness movement. Ideal for tweens, *Wonder* addresses common issues, such as bullying, friendship struggles, and the quest for popularity. This is a great way to broach these difficult topics and discuss real-life scenarios. You can also plan fun activities to go along with reading the book— making bookmarks, having book-themed snacks, and playing games related to the book.

Tip #3: Change the Way You Donate

If you're like most busy moms or stepmoms, once the children outgrow their clothing, you take it to Goodwill. This is great, but if you're going to donate, why not take it to a place that helps foster children or domestic abuse victims? Why not take your stepchildren with you, so they can see where their clothing is going and who will benefit from their clothes?

My stepdaughter is an only child and we only have her half of the time, so her clothes aren't worn very much before she outgrows them. Most of them look brand new. Instead of taking them to Goodwill, we take them to a place that helps foster children called Helen's Hope Chest. One time, the employee at Helen's Hope Chest gave us a tour and told us a little bit about what they do there and what the foster children need. We learned that some foster children have never received a birthday gift, so when they get to go into "John's Room" to pick out a new toy for their birthday, this is an extra special occasion for them. We also learned that the foster children get to pick out two books from the "Book Nook" and they get to pick out five outfits every three months. For a child that has everything, (technically, everything times two) like my stepdaughter, this was a great lesson in how something that means so little to us can mean the world to a foster child.

Tip #4: Volunteer

Volunteering can also provide your stepchild with another perspective, a glimpse into other people's daily struggles. You can volunteer at a soup kitchen or in a community garden. Finding age-appropriate volunteer opportunities can be hard, but if you have a Feed My Starving Children facility in your area, they offer volunteer tasks for all ages with parental supervision.

You can also create your own volunteer activity, simply by picking up trash in the park or in the neighborhood.

Tip #5: Encourage Small Acts of Kindness

Kindness can also happen in our neighborhood or in our community. It doesn't have to be formal, or planned weeks in advance. Make some cupcakes with your stepchildren, and then share them with your neighbors. If you have some extra vegetables in your garden, ask your stepchild to pick them and take them over to your elderly neighbor's house. These are all small acts of kindness that can brighten someone else's day. And your stepchildren can experience the joy that comes with bringing a smile to their neighbor's face.

Tip #6: Express Gratitude

Teaching our stepchildren to feel thankful and express gratitude to others is so important. Have your stepchildren write thank you notes to family members when they receive gifts. You can also encourage them to keep a gratitude journal. Another easy way is to make it a bedtime ritual to discuss a person or activity that made them feel grateful. Or have them write it on a whiteboard, which is a great reminder for them each day. According to research done by Dr. Martin Seligman, who runs the Positive Psychology Center, grateful people usually have more friends, more social interactions, and a positive view of life which helps them flourish. Isn't that precisely what we want for our stepchildren?

It starts with you...

These are just a few ideas on how to cultivate kindness and empathy in your stepfamily. If you repeat them over time, soon you will notice your stepchildren initiating them. Your stepchildren will automatically write thank you notes after their birthdays. They will ask if they can take those extra tomatoes from your garden over to the neighbor's house. Remember that repeating these small, consistent steps over time will lead to more empathetic children.

Small Steps Challenge: Try One of the Kindness Tips

Your challenge is to choose one of the tips above and try it with your stepchildren. If you can't actually complete it today because it requires more time, go ahead and make a plan for when you will do it.

Take it a Step Further...

Make sure you incorporate these tips into your stepfamily life over the next few months. Over time, you will notice a difference in how your stepfamily acts and how your stepchildren treat others.

Reflection

♥ Read the first tip again. What type of example are you providing? Are you modeling the kind of behavior you want to see in your stepchildren?

_____

_____

_____

_____

_____

♥ How did your stepchildren react? Did you notice any difference in their behavior?

_____

_____

_____

_____

♥ Is there anything you would do differently? What would you like to try in the future?

_____

_____

_____

_____

Day 13: Focus on your own happiness.

When we love ourselves, we naturally shine, and we are naturally beautiful. And that draws others to us. Before we know it, they're loving us, and it's up to us to choose who to share our love with.
—Kamal Ravikant

As stepmoms, we've got some big shoes to fill, and we are usually the ones who create those big shoes with all of our expectations of how we are going to excel as stepmoms. So let me ask you: are you feeling like you're doing everything? Going above and beyond? And to top it all off, no one appreciates what you're doing?

Take a minute and ask yourself: Why am I doing this?

Is it because you want to feel like you're the best stepmom? Is it because you want to prove to others that you're not an evil stepmom? Or is it simply because you think that's what being a stepmom means?

You'll be relieved to know this scenario is common among stepmoms, especially in the beginning. It is so common that there is a term for this behavior, and it's called ***over functioning***. It's an apt term, right? It conjures up images of a refrigerator operating above capacity and looking or sounding like it might blow up. Sound familiar? Do you feel like you might just have a nervous breakdown or "blow up" if no one acknowledges that thoughtful thing you did yesterday? It's useful to know that part of the reason why we're over functioning is because we are aware of the negative stereotype associated with stepmothers, and we are working hard to overcome that stereotype.

Trust me, I've been there. We all have! My story is the classic story of an over functioning stepmom. When I first became a stepmom, I stopped attending my weekly Zumba and yoga classes because I thought I needed to be home all the time. My husband and stepdaughter didn't have this expectation. I put this pressure on myself because I didn't want to be the selfish stepmom who only thought of herself. I also wanted to prove myself as a model stepmom to all of the volleyball moms, so I went above and beyond. I made special Halloween goody bags for all of the girls on the volleyball team. I went to every practice and game because I didn't want the other mothers to think of me as a wicked stepmother. However, rather than proving myself as Stepmother of the Year, I simply got burnt out trying to be the best I could. I reached my breaking point. I couldn't do it anymore. I didn't want to do it anymore. So I stepped back from some of the things I was doing, and I started to feel better.

So the important thing you should know about being an over functioning stepmom is that it can lead to stepmom burnout. That's why with all of the pressure that we put on ourselves, it's important to check out and take some time for ourselves in the form of self-care. Self-care is basically the idea that we need to take care of our own needs, so that we can be there to take care of others. That's why it's important to do things you are passionate about and enjoy doing. You will feel happier, and you can bring that happiness back to your partner or family.

It's not selfish to focus on your own happiness because your happiness affects those around you. Drastically. "A 30 percent increase in one spouse's happiness boosts the other spouse's happiness, while a drop in one spouse's happiness drags the other one down," according to Gretchen Rubin, author of *The Happiness Project*. This means that the happier you are, the happier your spouse will be, and vice versa. Since your marriage is the foundation of the stepfamily, it's essential to have a strong, healthy, and happy relationship. Be proactive– before you start feeling irritable, take a break. Go for a jog, take a nap, or meet your friend for brunch. You'll feel recharged and you can come back to your family with renewed energy. This is also a good opportunity for your husband to spend some time alone with his children.

Make sure that part of your self-care time includes time with a support group or friends. Time with a support group is ideal because you need to be able to talk to others who are in a similar situation. You can get valuable advice from others, and you can find out about stepfamily issues that you may encounter down the road. In fact, studies have shown if you have five or more friends with whom you could discuss an important issue, you're more likely to describe yourself as "very happy." This is crucial to us as stepmoms. With the everyday stressors that we're experiencing, it's important to have close friends or a support group to confide in. Making time for these friends or this support group should be a top priority for our own happiness.

You will also need to find stepmom friends or a stepmom group. Only fellow stepmoms can truly understand what you're experiencing because they're going through it themselves. We need to feel comfortable sharing how we are feeling without judgement. We can also get ideas and advice from each other, but keep in mind that everyone's situation is unique—with different problems, personalities, and feelings involved. When looking for a group, try to find one that is positive and supportive. While sometimes you might want to simply vent, it's not productive to complain or put undue focus on the negative aspects of being a stepmom without also looking for solutions and positive aspects.

Small Steps Challenge: Self-Care and Support System

Your challenge for today is two-fold.

First, plan one to two self-care activities in the next week. These self-care activities can include pampering activities, such as a facial or a massage, or they can be exercise-related, such as a hike or a run. Reading is also a good activity to relax and unwind. Just six minutes of reading per day reduces stress levels by 68 percent, according to a study by the University of Sussex in England.

The second part of this challenge is to find a stepmom friend or a stepmom support group. If you already have a stepmom friend, reach out and set up a coffee date or a brunch. If you need to find a stepmom group, do a quick search online or seek out resources at your local church or community center. Once you find a group, make a plan to attend a meeting.

In my experience with leading a stepmom group, I've found that the first meeting is usually the most difficult for stepmoms to attend. Typically, stepmoms feel nervous in the beginning, until they realize that they can safely share their experiences with others who understand them. One stepmom shared her feelings after the first meeting. "I've been stepparenting for six years, but I haven't sought out a group until recently. I really enjoyed the meeting yesterday and am already looking forward to next month's meeting. It was like looking into a mirror and conversation was easy. I felt so relieved." The most important thing is to find a group and then make a commitment to attend a meeting no matter how many excuses you have or how uncomfortable you feel the first time.

Reflection

♥ How much self-care time do you set aside per week? Do you feel like this is enough time? Do you feel yourself getting cranky or irritable after an "on" week?

_____

_____

_____

_____

_____

♥ How did you feel after your self-care activities?

_____

_____

_____

_____

_____

♥ How did you feel after your stepmom group meeting? What kinds of new ideas or perspectives did you gain?

_____

_____

_____

_____

_____

♥ Did you notice any differences in the dynamics of your marriage? Or your relationship with your stepchildren?

_____

_____

_____

_____

♥ What would you like to try next week?

_____

_____

_____

Day 14: Learn how to broach sensitive topics with your partner.

The goal in marriage is not to think alike, but to think together.
– Robert C. Dodds

You have probably already discovered that you need to be careful when you talk to your husband about his children. This is a common issue among stepmoms due to the delicate nature of the situation. Remember that your husband's children are an extension of him, so when you criticize them, no matter how small a criticism it might be, he views it as a criticism of him and his parenting style. Furthermore, odds are high that you have differing ideas of the best parenting style. According to a study done by Ron Deal and David Olson, this is an issue for 64 percent of unhappy stepcouples and 33 percent of happily married stepcouples. In general, men are protective of their children, so talking to them about their children can be an extremely sensitive issue for most men. For Shondra, a stepmom to one girl, communicating with her husband about his daughter proved to be one of the biggest stepparenting issues she had. Shondra shares her experience:

> When I talked to my husband about a discipline issue with his daughter, he would get defensive. Then I would get angry because I felt like he thought I was mean to his daughter. I also felt like he wasn't listening to me. Finally, after visiting a therapist, I realized the problem was actually in the way that I was bringing up the

issues. I had a tendency to be blunt and bring the issue up when I was angry. Instead, I learned how to talk to my husband in a more diplomatic way. I explained that what I was saying was coming from a place of love. From a place of wanting my stepdaughter to be the best person she could be. When I changed the way that I spoke to my husband, he didn't get defensive, and we could talk about the issue in a calm manner. It opened up our communication channels and made our marriage stronger.

When you need to talk to your husband about an issue related to his children, it is all about how you start the conversation. Dr. Gottman, a renowned marriage and relationship therapist, has found that how a partner raises an issue in the first three minutes of the conversation is critical to whether the couple is able to resolve relationship conflicts. Dr. Gottman recommends using a soft start-up, which means starting the conversation gently. Start by saying something positive, and then ask for your husband's input on how to solve the problem. "I love the creativity that Courtney put into the art project that she made. Unfortunately, she left all of her art materials out. How do you think we can get her to start picking up after herself without reminding her all the time?"

Or "I like the way Hayley has opened up to me and started talking to me about her friends and social life. The only problem is that she has started to talk back to me when I ask her about her homework. What do you suggest we do about this?" In this example, you are mentioning the bond that has developed between you and Hayley, but you are also pointing out an issue that you've been having. Now your husband has an opportunity to offer a solution, and he might offer to check up on academics. Then you can compliment him on how he supports you.

Contrast that with "I'm so fed up! Hayley was talking back to me again. Why don't you discipline her?" Inviting your husband to offer a solution or discuss an issue will generate a different response than if you start the dialogue with a criticism.

Alternatively, you can think of this communication tip as a "suggestion sandwich." Start with a compliment, make a suggestion, and then follow the suggestion up with a compliment.

Small Steps Challenge: Use a Soft Start-up

The next time an issue related to your stepchildren comes up, try using a soft start-up by sharing a positive comment before inviting your husband to offer a solution. Your challenge today is to try this technique with a minor issue, just so you can practice before you use it with topics that are more sensitive. If you feel angry about a situation, use the 24-hour rule and wait until you cool down to bring it up.

Take it a Step Further...

In the future, try a soft start-up when discussing issues with your husband. It'll take some time to get into the practice of doing it, but you'll notice a difference in your communication if you change the way you start the conversation.

Reflection

♥ What kinds of issues related to your stepchildren are difficult for you to broach?

_____

_____

_____

♥ How do you normally approach your husband about these issues? How does he react?

_____

_____

_____

♥ How did he react when you invited him to offer advice or a solution?

_____

_____

_____

Day 15: Connect with Your Partner

Any day spent with you is my favorite day. So, today is my new favorite day. —A.A. Milne

Our relationship with our partner is the most important relationship in the stepfamily because it provides the foundation for the stepfamily. Without a strong foundation, the stepfamily bonds will be shaky and unstable. And if it weren't for this relationship, you wouldn't be part of a stepfamily, so that's why it's important to nurture this relationship and put it first. The stronger your relationship is, the stronger your stepfamily as a whole can be. Plus, you can provide a good model of what a healthy, loving relationship looks like. You can connect with your partner in two crucial ways: through expressing appreciation and spending quality time together.

Expressing appreciation

According to a study conducted by Janice Kaplan, author of *The Gratitude Diaries*, "77 percent of men said they'd be grateful if their wives expressed love and affection." For men, having their wives show love and affection scored higher than making dinner, running errands, or planning a vacation. However, in this same study, less than half of women regularly expressed appreciation to their husbands, while 97 percent of women in the survey said that they would say thanks to a nice server in a restaurant. So what is going on here? Why would we express appreciation to a server when we don't say thanks to the person who is supposed to be closest to us? Part of it is due to what psychologists call *habituation*, which simply means that something that is novel to us in the beginning loses its allure as we become accustomed to it. This applies to things, such as a new car, and also to people. Think about when you first got married. Did you and husband act differently than you do now? Were you more grateful to him in the beginning than you are now? Part of it is due to habituation and part of it is due to our own expectations for our relationship. We start to take our partner for granted and just expect him to do all of the things that he is doing without thanks.

Small Steps Challenge: Try "Small Things Often"

It's time to take a very simple step to change that behavior. Take five minutes a day to focus on your partner. Dr. Gottman, marriage and relationship researcher, has a phrase he frequently uses in his couples counseling sessions. He encourages the idea of "small things often." This means it's not the big gestures that make a successful relationship. Rather, it's actually all the small things you do on a daily basis that contribute to a happy marriage, such as paying attention to your partner when he needs it, giving him a compliment, or noticing when he needs extra support.

Seahorses have this idea down pat. Most species of seahorses studied in the wild appear to remain faithful to one partner, forming pair bonds throughout a breeding season and perhaps even over multiple seasons. Pair bonds reinforce their relationship with a daily greeting–they dance together every morning before they part ways. This morning ritual is the perfect example of "small things often." You can practice "small things often" by leaving a note thanking your husband for making coffee and wishing him a nice day at work. Or you can send a quick text expressing appreciation for picking groceries up after a long day at work. It can be as simple as letting your partner know what you admire about him. Giving a compliment goes a long way–64 percent of unhappy couples struggle with putting each other down, while only 8 percent of happy couples have that issue, according to a survey by Ron Deal, author of *The Smart Stepfamily Marriage.*

You don't have to spend a lot of time on your partner, but you do need to make a conscious effort to set aside time for him every day. As you start putting this practice into place, you'll probably notice that your partner reciprocates by thanking you for what you do on a daily basis, giving you a compliment, or showing that he cares by leaving a note for you.

Spending quality time together

The other part of this equation is spending quality time together when you're just having fun with your partner. Are you getting enough quality time with your husband? Do you have regular date nights? Do you have time to talk to each other after the children go to bed? Of course, we'd like to answer "yes!" to all of these questions, but the reality is that it can be a struggle to get that quality time. Between work schedules, parenting schedules, and the demands of daily life obligations, our relationships can often fall to the bottom of our list of priorities. According to a study conducted by Ron Deal and David Olson, of the 50,000 couples they surveyed, 51 percent of the people wished that their partner had more time and energy for shared recreation or interests. Having a strong foundation with our partner is especially important in a stepfamily because we need that foundation, built on love, trust, and quality time, to give us the strength to handle day-to-day challenges. In fact, Deal and Olson discovered that shared leisure activity was the number four predictor of a happy, healthy marriage. That's why it's crucial to protect that time. However, you might need to get creative in order to get that quality time for your relationship.

Going on a weekend getaway or taking a vacation together may not be feasible with your parenting schedule, activities, or work demands. Plus, it can take a lot of planning! Instead of planning something elaborate, you can go on a microadventure with your partner. Some of you may be wondering what a microadventure is. The term was coined by adventurer Alastair Humphreys in 2012 and has been gaining in popularity ever since. According to Collins dictionary, a microadventure is an "adventure close to home." The New York Times provides an even better definition: "short, perspective-shifting bursts of travel closer to home." Sounds alluring, right? Who wouldn't want to go on a microadventure to reframe their current mindset and have a little fun in the process? A microadventure can be something as simple as trying a new Belizean restaurant and trying oxtail stew for the first time. Or it can be a trip to a planetarium to see a new laser light show. Maybe there is a charming town nearby where you can go horseback riding. These are all perfect examples of microadventures.

Now, I hate to make rules for something that is supposed to be fun, but it's necessary! There is actually only one rule for your microadventure, but it is a *very* important rule. Here it is: for parents and stepparents–don't talk about your kids, stepkids, or anything related to the stepfamily while you're on your microadventure. During your microadventure, it's just you and your partner. For these two or three hours, forget about everything else, and just enjoy the time together.

Small Steps Challenge: Plan a Microadventure

Your other challenge for today is to plan a microadventure for you and your partner. Ask your husband's opinion about what he'd like to do or just take charge and make a plan. Think about an activity nearby you've always wanted to try or a place your husband has mentioned. Then you can anticipate the day you'll actually go on your microadventure!

Take it a Step Further…

Practice both of these Small Steps Challenges on a regular basis. In the beginning, you will need to be intentional about planning and following through with them, but after a while, they will become second nature. Make sure to pencil in some potential microadventure dates on your calendar for the next few months. For your daily expression of appreciation and affection, you can get some special Post-it notes for your messages to your partner. (I have some lip-shaped ones that I use!)

Reflection

♥ How did your husband respond to your expressions of love, appreciation, and affection? Did he reciprocate?

_____

_____

_____

_____

♥ How much quality time do you normally have with your partner on a weekly basis? What kinds of things do you like to do together?

_____

_____

_____

_____

♥ How did your microadventure go? What was the best part of it?

_____

_____

_____

_____

Day 16: Have an attitude of gratitude.

If you change the way you look at things, the things you look at change.
–Wayne Dyer

One of my favorite habits that I started at the end of last year was writing in a gratitude journal. I had heard a lot about the benefits but hadn't bothered to try it myself. However, when I started to feel like I was focusing too much of my attention on negative things, I realized that I needed to shift my perspective and put my energy into thinking about all of the positive things happening in my life. For me, this meant starting to write in a gratitude journal every day. Stepmoms, if you notice you're focusing on the negative aspect of stepfamily life, like issues with your stepkids or their mom, it might be a good time to start your own gratitude journal.

Certainly, being a stepmom is not for the faint of heart. It's really easy to focus on negative things that have happened, and focusing on those negative aspects can affect our self-esteem over time. We may start to feel like we're failing or like we're to blame in the situation. Instead of focusing on those negative aspects, we need to keep building ourselves up to prepare for the next challenge by remembering all of the positive things that have happened that we might have simply overlooked. Now is the time to feel grateful for all of the things that have gone well.

According to an article in the *Journal of Social and Clinical Psychology*, gratitude may have the strongest connection to happiness of any of the personality traits studied. In fact, "18.5 percent of individual differences in people's happiness could be predicted by the amount of gratitude they feel," asserts Janice Kaplan, author of *The Gratitude Diaries*. Gratitude also has a positive effect on your health. Researchers have found that feeling gratitude can lower your blood pressure, help with depression, improve sleep, and reduce stress, according to Kaplan. That's why it's important for you to approach situations with an attitude of gratitude. Research on gratitude has shown that by finding the positive aspects of a frustrating experience, people can feel more positive about that experience. We can use ***grateful recasting***, a technique where people reframe or recast frustrations as opportunities and show gratitude for the moment, according to Robert Emmons, a leading expert on gratitude and author of *Thanks!: How Practicing Gratitude Can Make You Happier*.

As stepmoms, we encounter numerous frustrating situations, but that is where grateful recasting comes in— you can shift your perspective by focusing on all that you are learning through this experience. You are learning how to navigate difficult relationships, how to communicate, and how to handle tough situations, just to name a few. No, it is definitely not easy, but it has also shown you that you're a stronger person than you probably ever imagined yourself to be!

Small Steps Challenge: Start a Gratitude Journal

Your challenge is to incorporate a practice of gratitude into your daily life with a gratitude journal. You'll follow the steps below to get started and make your first entry today. We all have a finite amount of precious energy to expend each day. The beautiful part is we get to choose how we will expend that energy. Why not use that energy to focus on the positive things for which you are grateful in your life?

How to Start a Gratitude Journal

- **Find a notebook or a journal for your gratitude journal.** It doesn't have to be fancy, but if having a fancy one motivates you to write, by all means, go out and buy one!
- **Commit to a time period.** How many days will you be writing in your gratitude journal? You'll be more likely to follow through if you break it down into something manageable. You can start with one week or 21 days. You can always extend the time after you get started, but the key is (1) to get started and (2) to make it a habit.
- **Have an accountability partner.** Ask a friend, your mom, or your sister to join you in committing to write in a gratitude journal. You can ask them to hold you accountable for writing in it every day. I told my stepdaughter about my gratitude journal, and she wanted to start writing in one too, so we've been writing in our gratitude journals before bedtime. Sometimes we share what we wrote down with each other or with my husband. It's been a nice nightly ritual for us!
- **Write it down.** At the end of the day, think about your day and write down the person, thing, or event for which you are grateful and explain why you are grateful for them.

- It can be as simple as: I am grateful for _____ because _____.
- Here's an example: I am grateful for Romeo (my dog) because he's always so happy to see me when I get home. He cheers me up!

- **If it helps, take a photo each day of the things that you might write about in your journal.** This will help you to remember what happened during the day, and then you'll have a visual representation of your gratitude journal.

- **Reread what you wrote and allow yourself to feel grateful for the things, people, or events you wrote down.** Even if you have a bad day, you will see that you can still find one thing to be grateful for each day. This forces you to take your mind off your stressful commute or your bad day at work and focus on those things that brighten your life.

Take it a Step Further…

You can continue your practice of gratitude and make it part of your routine by writing in your journal three times a week. One stepmom, Kelley, shared how keeping a gratitude journal helped her. "I have a gratitude journal, and I always go back to it even if I leave it for a period of time. It's one of the most amazing tools I have. Each time I go to write something in it, I reread it from the beginning, and I feel like a whole new person!" Just like Kelley, you can always go back to your gratitude journal to give yourself a boost when you're feeling down. You can also write letters of gratitude or visit people to share your gratitude with them. Sharing your gratitude with others not only brightens someone's day, it also has a positive effect on your mood.

Reflection

♥ How did you feel after keeping the gratitude journal? Did you notice any difference in your attitude?

_____

_____

_____

_____

_____

♥What did you learn about yourself after reading through the gratitude journal?

_____

_____

_____

_____

_____

Day 17: Accept the things that are outside of your control.

Accept what you can't change. Change what you can't accept.
—Unknown

When you become a stepmom, you realize that so many things are outside of your control. The challenging part is being okay with not having control over so many things. Before you got married, you were in control of your household, your finances, and your time. When you marry into a stepfamily, you'll find that everything changes. You and your husband are in charge of the household, and you'll have to make financial decisions together. When you're planning holidays or vacations, you'll have to check with the other household to make sure you're not infringing on plans they've made.

The trap that many stepmoms fall into is **ruminating**, or brooding over, this loss of control. Women have a tendency to overthink things and to dwell on problems rather than solutions, which are examples of ruminating, according to Susan Nolen-Hoeksema, a psychologist at Yale. Women do a lot more ruminating than men because we are sociologically more inclined to put greater weight on our relationships with others, including our emotional connections. The danger with ruminating is that it can put us at risk for anxiety and depression. In fact, a study from McGill University in Montreal found that women produce 52 percent less serotonin in their brains than men do. This is important because serotonin is the hormone that manages our anxiety and keeps the amygdala, the fear center in our brain, under control. As a result, we have to make more of an effort than men to manage our anxiety and fears.

One of the most powerful ways to change the brain's structure and thought patterns is through meditation techniques. A number of studies that measured activity in the brain before and after mediation found less activity in the amygdala, the fear center in the brain, after an average of eight weeks of mediation, according to Katty Kay and Claire Shipman, authors of *The Confidence Code*. This means that one way we can manage our anxiety and fears is through a basic meditation practice.

Small Steps Challenge: Meditate

Today your challenge is to meditate for two to three minutes. Sarah Ortolf, who is a Usui Reiki Master, teaches meditation and mindfulness classes in Scottsdale, Arizona. She offers a quick tip for stepmoms who are feeling stressed and anxious. "Learning to become aware of your thoughts and feelings **before** the stress levels build up is so important! Just that awareness and acknowledgement, with a nice full breath, can change the entire way your emotions are functioning and stop the buildup before it starts to pile up."

When you're meditating, your goal is to clear your mind for a short period of time. As you start practicing meditation on a regular basis, you can slowly increase the amount of time you spend meditating. There are many different meditation techniques, but we're going to start with a simple one.

How to Meditate

- Find a comfortable place to sit or lie. You may want to dim the lights.
- Close your eyes and relax. Relax your jawbone, the area between your eyebrows, and your shoulders. Clear your mind. For the next two to three minutes, you are just going to focus on your breath.
- Don't try to control the breath. Just breathe naturally. Feel all of the tension leaving your body as you focus on your breath.
- Focus your attention on the breath and how your body moves every time you inhale and exhale. Feel your chest, shoulders, rib cage, and belly as you inhale and exhale. Just focus on your breath without trying to control your natural breathing patterns. If your mind wanders to what you need to do today or to your latest stressor, simply return your focus back to your breath.

Take it a Step Further…

In the beginning, meditating may be difficult. We are so accustomed to staying busy that it'll be tough to set aside time every week to meditate, but taking that time will pay off. Set aside those two to three minutes for five days a week, and then slowly increase it, so you are meditating for longer periods. You will feel more grounded and better able to handle stressors that emerge in your everyday life.

Small Steps Challenge: Focus on What You Can Control

Another technique when you are feeling like things are out of your control is focusing on what you can control. Marcus Aurelis, a philosopher, summed up this idea with this quote, "You have power over your mind–not outside events. Realize this, and you will find strength." Make a mind map or a list of what is in your control. Then when you're feeling powerless, take the mind map or the list out as a visual reminder. Here's an example of one:

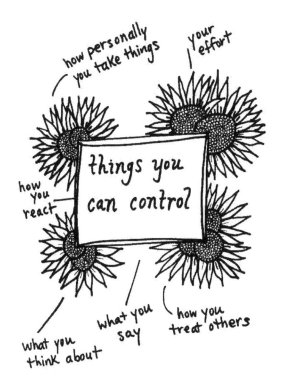

Take it a Step Further...

Make a series of *Things You Can Control* mind maps or lists for different areas of your life. You can make them for your home life and your work life. If you notice that your stepchildren are struggling with control, you can even encourage them to make one.

Reflection

♥ How did you feel after you meditated? Did you notice any difference in your mood?

_____

_____

_____

_____

♥ Take another look at your visual of *Things You Can Control*. Can you add anything?

_____

_____

_____

_____

Day 18: Focus on solutions rather than complaints.

What counts in making a happy marriage is not how compatible you are, but how you deal with incompatibility. –*Leo Tolstoy*

Conflict in a relationship is inevitable, but the important thing is how we are handling that conflict. Dr. John Gottman, marriage researcher, has discovered that 69 percent of problems in a relationship are unsolvable. You can refer to these as ***perpetual problems***—things like personality traits your partner has that irritate you, long-standing issues concerning parenting styles, or saving money. As you can imagine, trying to solve unsolvable problems is counterproductive, and no couple will be able to completely eliminate them. However, discussing them in a constructive way is helpful and provides a positive opportunity for understanding and growth. Gottman's research findings determined that couples must learn to manage conflict instead of trying to avoid or eliminate it.

When I think of conflict, I like to think of the 3 C's: communication, connection, and conflict. Good communication and a positive connection are important in order to come to a positive resolution during conflict. Take, for example, connection. There is a saying that goes, "I don't care how much you know until I know how much you care." Have you taken time to build a connection between you and your partner? Do you approach issues from the standpoint that you and your partner are on the same team? Open and honest communication is also crucial to how we resolve a conflict. Ron Deal and David Olson, marriage researchers and therapists, have discovered that communication is the number two predictor of couple satisfaction. In fact, when examining the factors that contribute to a happy relationship, communication makes up 35 percent. Finally, the way that we approach conflict is key. Instead of looking at conflict as a stumbling block, we should look at it as a stepping stone–as an opportunity for growth. By resolving conflicts, we learn how to work together as a team while also getting our needs met. That's why I refer to communication, connection, and conflict as the 3 C's– they are intertwined and they build on one another. We can transform our relationships by showing we care, communicating openly, and reframing our approach to conflict.

To do this, first we need to understand how people remember events. According to researchers, people are more likely to remember negative events than positive ones. Let me give you an example.

As an educator, at the end of a semester, I have equally conflicting emotions of both joy and dread. I'm excited to see how much my students have progressed during the class, but I'm also nervous about receiving my evaluations from the students. Did they learn a lot? Did they feel the same way about the class that I did? Most of the time, I receive glowing evaluations from happy students. But every now and then, I get one that is poor. Maybe the student thought I gave too much homework, or the tests were too hard. So I would have 19 positive evaluations and one negative one. Guess which one I focused on? Unfortunately, even with so many positive ones, I would focus on the negative one. This is just one example of how people are more likely to remember negative events than positive ones. Part of it is because of the way we process negative and positive emotions, according to Clifford Nass, a professor at Stanford University. Negative emotions tend to involve more ruminating, so they are processed more thoroughly than positive emotions. We also use stronger words to describe negative experiences than positive ones. That's why we are more likely to remember that time our passport was stolen while on vacation in Spain rather than the lovely day we spent at the beach. Or the time our family was talking loudly, and woke us up early on a Saturday morning, rather than the time they pitched in together to clean up the house.

How does this relate to our stepfamily life?

How often do you find yourself criticizing your stepchildren? What about your husband? Does it feel like you're complimenting them more than criticizing them? I hope you answered "yes" to that last question because researchers have found we need five positive interactions to outweigh each negative interaction during a conflict.

Dr. Gottman and Robert Levenson wanted to understand the difference between happy and unhappy marriages, so they conducted a series of studies on married couples. They asked the couples to solve a conflict in their relationship, and then they observed the couples for 15 minutes to see how they interacted with each other. After following up with the couples nine years later, they were able to predict with over 90 percent accuracy which couples would stay together. That's where that ratio of five positive interactions to one negative interaction during conflict comes in. Happy couples had a healthy ratio of positive to negative interactions, while unhappy couples had an unhealthy ratio, which typically led to divorce. While conflicts are inevitable, how couples treat each other during conflicts is one of the keys to a lasting relationship.

For everyday life, the ratio of positive interactions to negative interactions is even higher. The magic ratio for our day-to-day interactions is 20 positive interactions to every 1 negative interaction.

The results of these studies are also important for our interactions with our stepchildren. How are we handling conflict with them? When we're critical of them, are we also pointing out the things they did well? Are we hitting that 5:1 ratio with them during a conflict and the 20:1 ratio during our everyday life?

What qualifies as a negative interaction?

Negative interactions include eye-rolling, becoming defensive, and being critical. Ignoring someone or treating them in a dismissive way also count as negative interactions. We can counteract these negative interactions with positive ones, by expressing appreciation, being thoughtful, and complimenting our partner or stepchildren. A little kindness or empathy goes a long way when we're trying to solve a conflict with someone else. Just taking a moment to consider the issue from the other person's perspective can help us understand why that person might have reacted a certain way.

Small Steps Challenge: Try an "I care" Strategy

Your challenge is to work on maintaining this game-changing 5:1 ratio in your stepfamily. First, you'll want to take note of your interactions with your husband and stepchildren over a one-week period. Figure out your ratio of positive to negative interactions. If you do find yourself struggling with the positive interactions, then you'll want to be more intentional about incorporating positive interactions in your relationships. I have compiled a list of what I like to call "I care" strategies to help you get started. Your goal is to try at least one today.

I care...

1. Leave notes for your husband and stepchildren in their lunch or on the fridge.

2. Surprise them with a snack or a drink that you know they like.

3. Say "thank you" even for the little things.

4. Give hugs and kisses often.

5. Empathize with them. "What you're going through must be rough."

6. Make a special meal for them.

7. Listen to them. "What happened? Tell me more."

8. Spend quality time together. Go for a walk or a bike ride.

9. If you make a mistake, don't be afraid to apologize and admit you were wrong.

10. Give compliments.

11. Remember that you're on the same team. Be supportive when they're having a bad day.

Showing your stepchildren and your husband that you care about them is important to build a trusting and loving foundation for your relationship. You'll also want to remember these "I care" strategies when you're trying to solve a conflict. Even if you're arguing with your husband, by touching him on the arm, and saying, "I love you. This is hard for me to say, but I think this will help us in the long run," you can defuse tension and reassure your husband that you want the best outcome for you as a couple. Another benefit is once you start being intentional about practicing these "I care" strategies, you'll notice that your family members will follow your lead and start practicing them as well. Above all, remember the magic ratios of 5:1 during a conflict and 20:1 for everyday life, and your relationships within your stepfamily will be stronger.

Take it a Step Further...

Some other important reminders when resolving a conflict:

- First of all, remember the acronym HALT. Timing is important–never make any decisions or have big discussions when you're:

  Hungry

  Angry

  Lonely

  Tired

- Set a timer for five minutes to talk about one issue. Flesh out exactly what the issue is and both people should share their perspective or point of view.

- Set a timer for 5-10 minutes to brainstorm solutions. Your goal should be to focus on outcomes. You can determine this by asking yourself a simple question: What do I want? Instead of focusing on complaints, think about what you want from the situation. If you find yourself having an unhelpful dialogue that isn't going anywhere, leave it. You're not going to accomplish anything by forcing the issue.

- Instead, revisit it the next day when both of you have had time to calm down and cool off. You may want to give yourself 24 hours to think about it before you respond. Once again, the focus is on outcomes.

Reflection

♥ How was your ratio of positive to negative interactions with your partner? What about with your stepchildren? Did it surprise you?

_____

_____

_____

_____

♥ How did your partner or stepchildren respond to your "I care" strategy?

_____

_____

_____

_____

♥ Which strategies do you want to remember the next time you have a conflict with your partner?

_____

_____

_____

_____

Day 19: Disengage and set boundaries.

Take time to recharge your batteries. It is hard to see where you're going when your lights are dim. –Robert H. Connelly

Often, as a stepmom, you can start to feel like you're spinning your wheels. You might feel like you keep trying and trying without much luck. You might start to wonder, *Why should I even try?* Don't worry, it's normal to feel burnt out, and when you start feeling like that, it's time to step back and disengage.

You may find that a particular chore or activity is causing you stress and anxiety. You don't look forward to it and you really don't want to do it. So, why are you doing it? Stop! Stop right now. Don't worry–your husband and stepchildren will survive. You just need to let them know that you won't be doing that task anymore so they can plan on doing it themselves. Does your stepson keep complaining about how the clothes he wants to wear aren't washed? Let him know you won't be washing his clothes anymore. You can teach him how to do it or have your husband teach him how to do it. Now if his clothes aren't washed, he only has himself to blame. Does your stepdaughter keep giving you grief when you're trying to help her with her homework? Let your husband know you won't be helping her with her homework anymore. You don't need to make a big deal out of it, just let the person know in a calm manner what you won't be doing for them anymore. Jessica, a stepmom to two girls, shares her experience with disengaging.

> I felt a lot of stress and anxiety whenever I took my 10-year-old stepdaughter shopping. I

thought it would be fun, but every time we went, I got stressed out. Sometimes, she would spend a long time trying on clothes, insisting that she liked an outfit, but then she would never wear it. Other times, she would complain about not having clothing, but when I took her shopping, she would say she couldn't find anything. Every time I came back from shopping with my stepdaughter, I was frustrated and upset. My husband was not very understanding. "You're the adult. You make her try clothes on and wear them."

Finally, I decided to disengage. I told my husband and my stepdaughter I would not be taking her shopping anymore. That was the best decision I ever made! I didn't have to worry about whether my stepdaughter was wearing the clothes or not, and my husband understood what I went through the next time he took her shopping. This time, instead of trying to lecture me on how I should act when shopping with her, he lectured her on how to behave when shopping.

Just as Jessica's story illustrates, the key is identifying the activities that are causing stress, and then slowly disengaging from those activities. Once you choose a chore or activity, calmly let the other parties involved know that you won't be doing that activity anymore. Be prepared for some push back in the beginning, especially if it is something that you've been consistently doing. But you need to stay the course. After you disengage from doing that activity, re-evaluate the situation a couple weeks later. Do you feel better? Are there other activities from which you need to disengage?

Overall, remember that you're teaching others how to treat you. I love the quote, "What you will allow is what will continue." If your stepkids are not treating you with respect, you need to let them know and set some healthy boundaries. Ultimately, you get to choose how you spend your money and time, and you're in charge of your own happiness. If your stepchildren are not treating you with respect, you don't need to take them to the park or to that special activity you were planning. You can let them know you'll take them when they remember their manners. Just keep in mind that you don't need to constantly try to please them. It will put you in a bad mood when it doesn't go as planned. Don't let someone else determine how your day or your weekend is going to go—you're in charge of that.

The other part of disengaging is that when you disengage, you're setting healthy boundaries, and you'll have more time to spend doing things you love and enjoy. This will make you happier as a person and happier at home. You won't be that snappy stepmom who is getting frustrated and burnt out because she's feeling like no one appreciates what she does. It's easy to get overwhelmed as stepmoms and moms when trying to balance work and family obligations. Make sure you're saying "yes" to the things you want to focus on in your life. You'll want to be discerning with your "yeses" because every time you say "yes" you say "no" somewhere else.

In an extreme case, such as with a toxic relationship within the stepfamily that is harmful to you, you may need to disengage completely from a person. This is a decision that should not be taken lightly, and you'll want to take care of yourself during this difficult time. For instance, if your stepson is consistently putting you down, and it's affecting your self-esteem and overall wellbeing, then you can disengage from him completely. You can stop trying to please him. Instead, you can focus on your own life and do the things that you enjoy doing. You can let your husband know what you're doing and why. The important thing is that you need to protect yourself from these toxic relationships that can affect your self-esteem and drain your energy.

Small Steps Challenge: Disengage From an Activity

Today your challenge is to identify an activity that causes you stress and disengage from that activity. Let the involved parties know what you'll no longer be doing. Then make time for yourself a priority tonight and do one thing that makes you feel good.

Reflection

♥ How is your health and wellbeing in general? Are you suffering from anxiety or stress due to a certain activity?

_____

_____

_____

_____

♥ How did you feel after you disengaged from the activity? How did your husband and stepchildren react?

_____

_____

_____

_____

_____

♥ Are there other activities from which you need to disengage? Do you need to disengage completely from a stepfamily member?

_____

_____

_____

_____

_____

Day 20: Strive for progress, not perfection.

If there is no struggle, there is no progress. -Frederick Douglass

According to researchers, it takes about four to seven years for stepfamilies to blend. During this time, your stepfamily is evolving and growing, just as your relationship with your husband is. If you think back to when you first met, started dating, and got married, until now, you'll realize how many changes your stepfamily has gone through.

Jonelle Jones, a stepmom to four children, explains how her stepfamily evolved over the years.

> It seems like stepfamily relationships are constantly evolving, flexing and growing. I stepped very, very softly in the beginning of my relationship with the kids. We went at their pace. I was blessed in that they liked me from the start! But even then, the first few years were… 'weird' would be a good term. We were a family, but we didn't know each other. We spent a lot of time together, but we weren't bonded yet. It was an unusual place of being accepted by one another, but also not quite knowing what that meant.
>
> There was a noticeable evolution around year four as our connections became more authentic and our memories began to be shared. We were a little more relaxed around each other and had a lot of fun. They were also getting older and more interested in conversing about life, which

changed how we related to each other. It was fun to watch them grow! Looking back, I think I was still overly cautious with them. I dreaded making a wrong move, but to them I'd been around a long time and wasn't going anywhere. They'd accepted me into their family, but I was so scared of failing them that I kept more distance than I probably needed to.

In the last year, we went through another noticeable evolution. It's like we all let out a big exhale. Now everything is 'normal'. What I mean by that is, we are a family and we'd all tell you that matter-of-factly. We're comfortable with each other, I've gotten more comfortable in my stepmom role, and we've built a shared life together. We still deal with the complexities of stepfamily life, but we've learned how to do so with minimal discomfort.

Jonelle's story illustrates how long it can take stepfamilies to figure each other out and start to bond. As stepmoms, we tend to be cautious in what we say and do since the bond is fragile in the beginning. I liken it to walking on a suspension bridge. As you're walking across the bridge, you can feel the bridge swaying back and forth. You slow your pace and try to stay balanced as the bridge is moving below your feet. You're making progress, but it takes longer to cross the bridge, and you have an unsteady feeling as you're going across. It takes strength and resolve to make it to the other side. This is a perfectly natural feeling when you are traversing a shaky bridge or navigating a fragile relationship.

Of course, each stepfamily will have its own set of challenges depending on the dynamics of the situation. According to Dr. Patricia Papernow, author of *Surviving and Thriving in Stepfamily Relationships: What Works and What Doesn't*, children under eight years old have an easier time adjusting to being part of a stepfamily than older children. In addition, boys have an easier time than girls. In fact, teenage and pre-teen girls have the hardest time adjusting to a stepfamily. Allison, a stepmom to one girl, shares her story about when she first got married.

> Since my husband was a single dad for a couple of years before we got married, he was accustomed to taking care of Ashley, his seven-year-old daughter, on his own. They were a team. They did everything together. From deciding on what to have for dinner to deciding what to do on a Saturday afternoon, they made all of their decisions jointly. She slept in his bed and sat next to him at the dinner table. When we got married and I was thrown into the mix, this balance was thrown off. Ashley was used to having her dad to herself and making all of the decisions with him. My husband was used to consulting Ashley about dinner or weekend plans. I, on the other hand, was accustomed to the way that I was raised, with my parents making the decisions and us, as children, going along with those decisions. Suddenly, Ashley had a stepmother who was part of the decisions. My husband had another person to consult. And I was often frustrated when my husband would

ask Ashley if she wanted to do an activity that I had planned or if she wanted to eat at a certain place for dinner. Her answer was often 'no.' Instead of being a child, she seemed like an adult from the time that I met her because her parents treated her like an adult. They asked what she would like for dinner, what she would like to do each day, and which school she wanted to attend. Consequently, she did not appreciate the decisions that we made without consulting her.

Allison's story illustrates a common issue. A typical scenario among divorced dads, especially for those who were single for a long time, is elevating their daughter to a spousal position, called the *Mini-Wife syndrome*. When dad was single, his whole life revolved around his daughter, so she is accustomed to receiving all of the attention. She may become jealous when her dad shows physical affection to her stepmom. She may try to come between her dad and stepmom when they are holding hands, or try to sit on his lap when they're sitting next to each other. She might feel like she has the right to be included in decisions that are more appropriate for adults. These are all signs of a stepdaughter who may be exhibiting Mini-Wife syndrome.

To combat this, you and your husband will need to talk about the appropriate roles for each family member. This is when you'll want to revisit the rules and expectations that you set on Day 7 of the challenge. You'll also want to practice your communication skills by using a soft start-up to bring this topic up to your husband. Remember that the focus should be on what's best for your relationship as a couple so you can have a strong foundation for your stepfamily. You can also explain to your husband that you want your marriage to be a good model for your stepdaughter and how she can expect to be treated in her own marriage in the future.

As for Allison, she brought this difficult topic up to her husband. "I talked to my husband about how we, as parents, should be able to make plans without consulting Ashley first. Slowly, we have made progress. My husband no longer cooks a special meal for Ashley. Ashley sleeps in her own bed and I sit next to my husband during mealtimes. At times, to me, it seems like a slow process, but when I look back at how things used to be, I realize that we have made progress and that's what counts."

This is one example of how difficult situations can be resolved over time by using effective communication skills and conflict management strategies. You've probably had other situations arise in which you had the opportunity to experiment with your communication and conflict skills. Being a stepmom requires a great deal of patience and willingness to overcome obstacles. Think about how much you've learned and how far your family has come throughout the course of your stepfamily journey. And the best news is that family researchers have found that nine years down the road, children in stepfamilies look very much like children in first-time families, according to Dr. Papernow. This should be comforting to you as you think about the future of your stepchildren and your stepfamily in general.

Small Steps Challenge: Make a Timeline

Make a little timeline or a list of changes that have occurred in your stepfamily over time. You might be surprised by how much progress has been made. Start from when you got married and consider the positive changes that have occurred. Here is a list of topics to help you remember some of those events:

- discipline
- rules/expectations/consequences
- chores
- the dynamics with the ex-wife
- roles within the family
- new house/new school

Reflection

♥How have the relationships within your stepfamily changed or evolved over time? What has been the most positive change to date?

_____

_____

_____

♥ How have you changed or grown as a person? What are some of the important lessons you've learned?

_____

_____

_____

Day 21: Keep working on your plan.

What you do every day matters more than what you do every once in a while. —Unknown

What's next? Keep writing, reflecting, and challenging yourself on a daily basis. Repeat some of the small steps you've taken. Your strength will lie in being resilient and bouncing back after the low points. One week, everything may be going exactly as planned, and the next week you'll feel like you're about to pull your hair out. The good news is that you're always learning and becoming a better person in the process.

No matter what happens, you need to protect your precious energy and use it in ways that benefit you. You have a limited amount of energy, and you'll want to use your energy with intention. Think about where you're currently using your energy, and whether you're using your energy to grow or whether you're using it for things that sap your energy.

Important questions to ask yourself:

- Who or what deserves my best energy?
- Who or what matters most?

Your answers to these questions should guide you as you're making decisions. Furthermore, as life changes, you will need be flexible and go with the flow. At the end of each week, you should evaluate:

- Where you are
- What you need to work on

Although this is the last official day of the boot camp, your challenge is ongoing. Continue to look at your role as a stepmom as a project that you need to work on and refine. As Brené Brown says, "This journey is yours alone, but no one goes it alone."

Small Steps Challenge: Revisit Your Goals

Today your challenge is to go back to the goals you made on Day 2. What do you need to change or add to your goals? Look over your goals and make new goals for this week. Remember what consumes your mind, controls your life. What do you want to focus on? Use the visualization of your future self that you discovered on Day 2 to help guide you as you're making new goals. Remember to think about where you want to be in 20 years and the steps that you need to take to get there.

Take it a Step Further…

Buy a journal or a planner and start keeping track of your weekly goals. This will be a great way for you to track your progress over time and to constantly motivate yourself to improve the parts of your life you can control.

Your journey doesn't end here. Connect with our stepmom community and gain access to resources by visiting us at www.TheStepmomProject.com. You'll be part of a community who will laugh, cry, and empathize with you.

Reflection

♥ How have you changed throughout this challenge? In which areas do you feel stronger? Which ones do you need to continue to work on?

_____

_____

_____

_____

♥ What was the best thing that happened to you on your journey? What was the biggest lesson you learned?

_____

_____

_____

_____

♥ What's next for you on this journey? What are you anticipating?

_____

_____

_____

_____

Suggestions for Further Reading

Adventures for Your Soul by Shannon Kaiser

Braving the Wilderness by Brené Brown

Constructive Wallowing by Tina Gilbertson

Daring Greatly by Brené Brown

Expressive Writing: Words that Heal by James W. Pennebaker and John F. Evans

Girl, Wash Your Face by Rachel Hollis

Love Yourself Like Your Life Depends on It by Kamal Ravikant

Meditations by Marcus Aurelis

Playing Big: Practical Wisdom for Women Who Want to Speak Up, Create, and Lead by Tara Mohr

Rising Strong by Brené Brown

Stepmonster by Wednesday Martin

The Compound Effect by Darren Hardy

The Confidence Code by Katty Kay and Claire Shipman

The Gratitude Diaries by Janice Kaplan

The Happiness Project by Gretchen Rubin

The Happy Stepmother by Rachelle Katz

The Smart Stepfamily Marriage by Ron L. Deal and David H. Olson

Made in the USA
Middletown, DE
14 June 2021

42236058R00083